T0078139

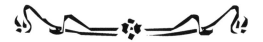

LADIES,
It Is Time to Get Smart

*Think Smart and Act Smart
to Become the Very Best*

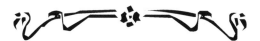

HAZEL L. WHITE, PHD

WESTBOW
PRESS®
A DIVISION OF THOMAS NELSON
& ZONDERVAN

Scriptures marked KJV are taken from the KING JAMES VERSION (KJV): KING JAMES VERSION, public domain.

Scripture quotations are from the ESV® Bible (The Holy Bible, English Standard Version®), copyright © 2001 by Crossway, a publishing ministry of Good News Publishers. Used by permission. All rights reserved.

WestBow Press books may be ordered through booksellers or by contacting:

WestBow Press
A Division of Thomas Nelson & Zondervan
1663 Liberty Drive
Bloomington, IN 47403
www.westbowpress.com
1 (866) 928-1240

Because of the dynamic nature of the Internet, any web addresses or links contained in this book may have changed since publication and may no longer be valid. The views expressed in this work are solely those of the author and do not necessarily reflect the views of the publisher, and the publisher hereby disclaims any responsibility for them.

Any people depicted in stock imagery provided by Thinkstock are models, and such images are being used for illustrative purposes only. Certain stock imagery © Thinkstock.

ISBN: 978-1-5127-7238-8 (sc)
ISBN: 978-1-5127-7240-1 (hc)
ISBN: 978-1-5127-7239-5 (e)

Library of Congress Control Number: 2017901177

Print information available on the last page.

WestBow Press rev. date: 3/20/2017

DEDICATION

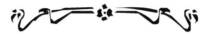

This book is dedicated to all women who are trying to find their way in a world that is dominated by men. We must remember that we are smart and can achieve our place.

ACKNOWLEDGMENTS

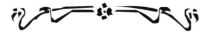

God is the inspiration for all that I do. I give Him praise for guiding me as I move toward being His representative here on earth. People should see Jesus in us. This is one of the ways that lost people are able to get to know Jesus. This is an awesome responsibility for Christians. I pray that we are able to meet the challenge.

Special appreciations go to Pastors Troy D. and Nicole King of The Glory Has Come International Ministries in Kannapolis, North Carolina. They have been a tremendous spiritual support for me and my family.

Finally, my five grandchildren keep me striving every day. They are Jahlen Kareem Lee (eleven years old), Keri JaNae Lee (seven years old), Kori Jade Lee (six years old), Hazeleigh Jael Robinson (three years old), and Hezekiah Jacoby Seeden (twenty-two months old). Their mothers, Jessica and Jennifer, are always dear to me.

CONTENTS

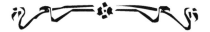

PREFACE

If you don't make the time to work on
creating the life you want, you're eventually
going to be forced to spend a *lot* of time
dealing with a life you *don't* want.

—Kevin Ngo, *Let's Do This!*

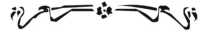

B y nature, most women have a desire to nurture. Women
love taking care of family and friends. They want to help
as many people as they can. Some women are worse than
others. They seem to make a life of looking for the people who
are down on their luck. They spend too much time in rescuing
and lifting up other people who do not try to lift up themselves.
Most of their focus is on men. Also, there seems to be no focus
on themselves. For some women, it is rarely a focus on children,
church work, school volunteerism, community service, and similar
endeavors. The good thing is that these focuses are positive and
they do not hurt women. In these situations, the people involved
seem to appreciate the women's efforts. Note that this writer is not
bashing men. The truth just needs to be told. It is not uncommon
to see men who do not appreciate your help. They often show their
appreciation by establishing new relationships with other women
or leaving you for younger or more desirable women.

Ladies, it is time for you to start nurturing yourselves. You
have to stop feeling sorry for yourselves. You have to overcome

your depression and self-defeating behaviors when things do not work out. If you spend more time nurturing yourselves instead of nurturing a man, you can become more educated, informed, interesting, impressive, attractive, politically active, admired, confident, self-assured, and other desirable attributes. It is never too late to pull yourselves together. The information you need is out there. You must look for it and apply it to your everyday lives.

You live in the Information Age. There is no excuse to be limited in information about every avenue of life, unless you cannot read or hate to read. Of course, one has to work on that terrible habit. You will be missing out on a lot of life information. The Information Age is also known as the Computer Age, Digital Age, or new media age. The onset of the Information Age is associated with the Digital Revolution, just as the Industrial Revolution marked the onset of the Industrial Age" (https://en.wikipedia.org/wiki/Information_Age).

Even though the terms *Computer Age, Digital Age,* and *New Media Age* may be used interchangeably when discussing the subject in general conversation, they may have some minor differences. Therefore, let us define them to make sure we are talking about the same thing and keeping everything in the proper perspective when we refer to them. First of all, let us take a brief look at the term *Computer Age.* The Computer Age is "the period in modern history characterized by computer use and development and its effects on all aspects of life" (http://dictionary.reference.com/browse/computer%20age).

It is shocking to the older generation to see how the world has changed with the onset of computers. It has changed the way we do business, from banking and paying bills to purchasing and selling goods. It has changed management of the household, workplace, church, and community, as well as methods of communication and other aspects of life. It has also changed the type and amount of work that can be done at home as opposed to at work. All home appliances, automobile parts, and office equipment have computer chips in them. The computer chips and computer components can be seen in the following but are not limited to them: refrigerators, stoves, microwaves, dishwashers, vacuum cleaners, alarm systems, televisions, cameras, telephones, various recorders, watches, and clocks, and the list goes on. Do not forget the toys. Some of these items have computer chips or computer components. These include talking and mobile stuffed animals and dolls, trains, cars, airplanes, playhouse items, and others.

"The Digital Age, also called the Information Age, is defined as the time period starting in the 1970s with the introduction of the personal computer with subsequent technology introduced providing the ability to transfer information freely and quickly" (http://www.yourdictionary.com/digital-age). With the advent of the computer, we can write and publish theses, dissertations, books, newspapers, and other forms of information faster. At the same time, we can get information faster for job training courses, certification and licensure courses, and general and specialized continuing education.

The term *New Media Age* "most commonly refers to content available on-demand through the internet, accessible on any digital device, usually containing interactive user feedback and creative participation. Common examples of new media include websites such as online newspaper, blogs, wikis, video games, and social media. A defining characteristic of new media is dialogue. New media transmit content through connection and conversation. It enables people around the world to share, comment on, and discuss a wide variety of topics. Unlike any of past technologies, new media is grounded on an interactive community" (https:// en.wikip edia. org wiki/new_media).

There are several resources available to us. Let us take a brief look at these. For those of you who have limited knowledge about this subject, this is a brief overview and introduction. You can take courses and read books to get a better understanding. This is written to let you know that there are resources available to you.

The Internet

The internet hosts a wealth of information on all possible subjects. All you need is time. There are online courses and training programs.

You can learn a foreign language. You can learn to cook. You can learn to play the piano. This list goes on. If you want to learn something new or get information to help you with homework, go to the internet. Do not forget YouTube. There are lessons on just about every topic, from algebra to zoology. It is out there. You can start your self-taught mission today.

Television Programming

There are a number of television programs that address common problems experienced by women. These programs cover topics related to relationships, child rearing, finances and wealth, health, employment, politics, faith, and social concerns. This information is provided on reality shows, talk shows, documentaries, court or judge shows, and local and national news programs.

Social Media

Social media may be defined as "computer-mediated tools that allow people to create, share, or exchange information, ideas, and pictures/videos in virtual communities and networks" (https://en.wikipedia.org/wiki/Social_media). It may also be defined as "a group of Internet-based applications that build on the ideological and technological foundations of Web2.0, and that allow the creation and exchange of user-generated content."

Daniel Nations (n.d.) listed the following as examples of common social media websites (http://webtrends.about.com/od/web20/a/social-media.htm):

- **Social Bookmarking** (Del.icio.us, Blinklist, Simpy): Interact by tagging websites and searching through websites bookmarked by other people.
- **Social News** (Digg, Propeller, Reddit): Interact by voting for articles and commenting on them.

- **Social Networking** (Facebook, Hi5, Last.FM): Interact by adding friends, commenting on profiles, joining groups, and having discussions.
- **Social Photo and Video Sharing** (YouTube, Flickr): Interact by sharing photos or videos and commenting on user submissions.
- **Wikis** (Wikipedia, Wikia): Interact by adding articles and editing existing articles.

Nations further stated that these websites are not the only social media websites. Any website that invites you to interact with the site and with other visitors falls under the definition of social media.

Magazines and Newspapers

Magazines and newspapers are popular reading materials. According to the Newspaper Association of America, nationally, over fifty-six million newspapers are sold daily (http://www. libraryspot.com/ know/newspaper.htm). Additionally, on Sundays, over sixty million are sold. Basically, magazines are publications that are printed or electronically published. (The online versions are called online magazines.) They are generally published on a regular schedule and contain a variety of content. They are generally financed by advertising, by a purchase price, by prepaid subscriptions, or a combination of the three.

Books

If you have spent a minute breathing, you know what a book is and how it expands our knowledge. There are so many secrets in books. The Bible is one of those that almost everybody has heard of. "The Bible is widely believed to be the best-selling book of all-time, with Guinness World Records estimating that over five billion copies have been sold" (https://en.wikipedia.org/wiki/ List_of_best-selling_books). It was also stated that *"Quotations from Chairman*

Mao Tse-tung and the Qur'an are also widely reported to be some of the most printed and also some of the most distributed books worldwide, with billions of copies of each of them believed to be in existence." We must understand that the exact print figures for these and other related books may also be missing or unreliable, since these kinds of books may be produced by many different and unrelated publishers, in some cases over many centuries. The books of a religious, ideological, philosophical or political nature have been excluded from many lists of best-selling books for these reasons.

Every topic of interest can be found in a book somewhere. Most of our knowledge came from books. Books are widely used in schools around the world. They are most often available for free to the students or interested readers in the schools, public, and governmental libraries. Books can be purchased from well-known book stores such as these:

- Barnes and Noble
- Book Off USA
- Books-a-Million
- Deseret Book (also operates Seagull Book)
- Family Christian Stores
- Follett's
- Half Price Books
- Hastings Entertainment
- Hudson News (chiefly located at airports and train stations)
- Joseph-Beth Booksellers (also operates Davis-Kidd Booksellers in Nashville and Memphis)
- Powell's Books, which includes the world's largest independent new and used bookstore
- Schuler Books and Music
- LifeWay Christian Resources

Many communities have bookstores. In these bookstores, you have a hands-on experience in exploring a number of books. Additionally, books may be ordered online. A full list may be found at http://www.scaruffi.com/fiction/booksell.html. Some of the well-known sites for purchasing books include the following:

- Amazon.com
- Barnes and Noble
- BiblioBytes; Hoboken
- Books-a-Million
- Book Stacks Unlimited (Cleveland, Ohio, USA)
- Books and Bytes, Inc. (Naperville, Ilinois, USA)
- Creation (specialty Christian bookstore)
- Half Price Books
- The McGraw-Hill Bookstore (New York, USA)
- Read USA
- Simon and Schuster's SuperStore
- Textbookland

There are also available websites that have lists of must-read book titles. For example, Megan Willett (2014) has a list of "100 Books Everyone Should Read Before They Die" (http://www. business insider.com/amazons-100-books-everyone-must-read-2014-2). Many of the books on her list are twentieth-century classics or recent bestsellers. There are other guides out there, including book lists from schools and universities.

Personal Notes from the Author

I can remember the times that I did not treat myself well. I grew up during a time when people were discriminated against based on a number of superficial attributes that included skin color, race, age, gender, disabilities, weight, and looks. Do not get me wrong—discrimination still exists today. It is definitely different today. It is still especially an issue during childhood. Children can be mean. This can lead to the type of bullying that many children encounter. Bullying has taken on a special adaptation with computers and other communication devises. There was some bullying when I was a child. Bullying has been an issue for many generations.

For some reason, today it appears to be occurring on a larger scale, leading children to suicide. The ultimate consequence is that these events can have a negative impact on a child's self-esteem. Furthermore, these issues can lead to depression, low self-esteem, distorted body image, relationship problems, and general lack of success.

Television, movies, and magazines demonstrate what beauty is supposed to look like. Additionally, these media demonstrate the expected roles of women. If you do not fit the expected pattern, you were not considered beautiful or a traditional woman. Things have gotten so much better now. Now, women have more options. Additionally, if you are a little different or want something different, you can do your thing or just be you.

As a child, I was ridiculed for doing well in school. They called me a bookworm. I have not really understood why children who do their schoolwork and more are ridiculed. They should be admired. Of course, you will be admired later in life. It will come for you, as it has for me.

I was not the best-dressed girl in school. I had new, well-fitting, clean, and neat clothes. They were not fancy or fashionable items. I asked my mother for what I thought would be better clothes. My mother asked me to choose between being the best-dressed or being the best educated. She said that we could not afford both. We had to plan and save for a college education. Well, I chose education. I took piano lessons and traveled a lot to enhance my background, which was something that my classmates did not have. At the time, I did not realize that children will try to demean or bully others even if they have good experiences or are doing well. I had to learn that jealousy can cause children to behave in this manner.

With all that said, I thought that I had the problem. It was years later before I realized that they had the problem. Because I did not have close friends while I was young, I learned to entertain and amuse myself. I read a lot about many different kinds of people from all backgrounds, histories, countries, cultures, places, events, and religions. I enjoyed stories about biblical characters, romances, professions, and other topics. I believed that I became well-rounded through reading. I gained a true respect and tolerance for all people. Also, I gained a wealth of general knowledge that has been very useful in my life. This turned out to be a great thing for me.

One of my favorite songs to help me cope with some of things that happened to me is entitled "Turn Back the Hands of Time," which was sung by Tyrone Davis. I know that I am telling my age. Of course, he was talking about a love relationship gone bad. I used the phrase to refer to mistakes, missed opportunities, failed efforts, and love relationships gone bad. We cannot turn back the hands of time. We have to learn to forgive ourselves and others and move on. I say to all of you, forgive yourselves and others and move on. It is never too late to make a change. There are other opportunities. There are new experiences waiting to happen. There are new people to meet. You can learn new knowledge and skills. It is not too late to go back to school. It is not over until God says it is over. Just open your mind and heart to these new opportunities and experiences. You cannot live your life in fear of change. Remember these words:

> You gain strength, courage, and confidence
> by every experience in which you really stop
> to look fear in the face. You must do the
> thing which you think you cannot do.
>
> —Eleanor Roosevelt

Also, try these words of encouragement:

> Try a thing you haven't done three times.
> Once, to get over the fear of doing it. Twice,
> to learn how to do it. And a third time to
> figure out whether you like it or not.
>
> —Virgil Thomson

CHAPTER 1

Who Are Your Teachers?

The start is what stops most people.

—Don Shula

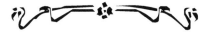

The messages and lessons are out there. Are you listening? Remember that this is the Information Age. If you want to know or learn it, you can find it. There is no excuse for the lack of knowledge. It is all about what you want and what you want to accomplish.

There are many resources out there that can help you achieve your dreams, desires, and goals. All of us are not equally endowed with equal resources; however, we can all find the resources that we need. Getting started is the key.

It does not matter when and where you start. It is about where you are going, how you plan to get there, and arriving at your chosen place. Having faith in God and yourself will take you there. Never give up. Only losers give up.

Parents

Your first teachers are your parents or guardians. Most parents and guardians try to teach values (whether good or bad), survival skills, social skills, self-care skills, and a variety of general knowledge to their children. They teach about culture, religion, appropriate behavior, family, and community. They do this by direct teaching (talking to them) or modeling skills for children to imitate (demonstrating the appropriate behavior). A wealth of knowledge is exchanged between children and parents. It is obtained during the most critical years of life, from birth to school age. This is an awesome responsibility. Some parents are very good at it. My parents were excellent teachers. Their lessons are still relevant to me, and I adhere to many of them. Then, there are parents who need help. Most communities offer parenting classes to help them. Check with the Department of Human Services, Family Services, or similar organizations for this valuable assistance for yourself or to recommend for love ones.

It is essential for parents or guardians to learn as much as they can about how to teach their children. Such topics as religion and prayer have been eliminated from school. Parents and guardians must pick up the slack. Many cultural and related heritage topics may be missing from the school's curriculum. Sex may not be adequately taught, and sex education classes based on family and religious values are often missing unless it is a religious school. There is a lot to be learned at school, but there is a lot of information that will not be learned at school. It is our responsibility to learn about these important issues and teach our children. We cannot leave this responsibility to others and the streets.

Ministers

Many people are exposed to religious teaching at an early age. Ministers are typically the second-most important teachers who influence a child's knowledge, attitudes, behaviors, and skills before the child attends school. Depending on the level of education and skills of the minister, people are profoundly impacted by his or her teachings. Today, ministers are expected to address many issues that are excluded from the academic curriculum. For example, they teach on such topics as these:

- faith
- morals

- sex
- family
- relationships
- finances
- life after death
- abortions

The Bible

The greatest book of all time is the Bible. It has "been a major influence on literature and history, especially in the West where it was the first mass-printed book" (https://en.wikipedia.org/wiki/Bible). It has often been used as one of the textbooks in many schools from early history. It has been translated into many languages. According to a statistical summary provided by *UBS World Report,* March 2002, "the total Bible has been translated in approximately 2,287 languages based on seven regions" (http:// www.biblica.com/en-us/bible/bible-faqs/how-many-different-languages-has-the-bible-been-translated-into/). So, the Bible is available for many people around the world. Many churches and organizations in your area may give you a free Bible. The next option is to purchase one online, in a bookstore, or in a large department store. It does not have to be expensive. You should make sure the print is easy for you to see and read.

Schoolteachers

Free education (public education) is available for all Americans. In fact, most states require children to go to school for a number of years. This may vary from state to state. The value of education is instilled by the parents or guardians. The schools or supervised homeschooling programs are vital to achieving essential academic knowledge in reading, arithmetic, and writing leading to advanced skills in preparation for college, vocational schools, the military, and other endeavors. Most careers require a high school diploma or its equivalent. Also, many public schools and colleges offer certain training for trades for free or for a very small fee. It is worth taking time to investigate the possibilities and get started in planning your education, if you do not have a high school diploma.

Children learn a lot from their teachers, whether directly (through instruction) or through modeling and imitation. Parents and guardians must become involved in their children's education in order to know what is going on. Just as in any profession, there are good teachers and those who fall short. The ones who fall short must be identified and dismissed. Schooling is too short in time to learn a massive amount of information. Teachers must be knowledgeable and skillful enough to get this done during the allotted time.

Most of us depend on the school to do a great job. Most parents have to work jobs. Sometimes, they must work two jobs to keep a roof over their children's heads, food on the table, and clothes on their backs. It is also difficult to find the needed funds to provide your children with additional educational tutoring programs. As a result, parents expect teachers to help them and their children.

At an early age, children love their teachers and try to please them. They are willing to learn and work hard. They need the support of the family. Parents must show their support and express respect for the teachers and the schools. If parents do not respect and support the schools, the children will learn to disrespect and not support the schools. A child's life will be devastated, if he or she does not receive a good education. He or she may be limited in employment opportunities, resources for health care, housing options, living conditions, and chances for building wealth. Most logically thinking parents and guardians want the best for their children.

It is never too late for adults to change their educational outlooks. There are many adult classes available in many communities. You can earn a high school diploma and a college degree online. The present economy requires an individual to stand out in a crowd. Certain knowledge and skills will keep you working. For example, people in the medical fields, especially nursing, can always find a job. It may be necessary to change professions or retool your skills. It is up to you.

College Teachers

Some of us are blessed with the opportunity to advance our education past high school. A college or university education can offer tremendous life-changing experiences. First, you get an opportunity to meet and know people from diverse backgrounds, races, cultures, nationalities, lifestyles, religions, worldviews, opinions, attitudes, values, and personalities, and the list goes on. From these experiences, you will learn tolerance and compassion for people who are different from you.

Second, you will learn a wealth of knowledge and skills. You will learn from teachers who bring various backgrounds, knowledge, and skills to the table. They are typically interested in your learning and more. They are compassionate, understanding, patient, helpful, and willing to share.

Third, the networking opportunities are endless. You make friends and associates who may be able to help you in the future. You can join nationally and internationally recognized organizations that can also help you in the future. These organizations may represent honor societies in your field of study and social fraternities and sororities. You can also become a member of organizations related to your future practice disciplines, including groups for future teachers, nurses, engineers, medical professionals, artists, writers, psychologists, counselors, writers, scientists, and many others. These connections are priceless.

Environmental Observations

Not only are we to learn from mistakes in our own lives, but we must also remember that we cannot keep on making the same mistakes that our friends and families are making. That is not smart.

We make many mistakes that should not have happened. We

see people attempt to do a certain act and fail. Why would we try the same thing? Do we think that we are smarter? Are cigarette smoking, drinking alcohol, and taking drugs addictive only to other people? Does sex without protection lead to sexually transmitted diseases only for other people?

The Television Judges and Talk Shows

There are many court and talk shows on television. You can learn a lot of interesting information from them. You have a chance to see people in serious situations that you may have experienced and situations that you are warned to avoid. You may also possibly learn how to get help. These are supposed to be real cases and incidents. It is unbelievable that people find themselves in situations that thousands of people have already experienced. They observed the consequences of others getting into these situations. However, they chose to try these for themselves, as if the consequences would not happen to them.

We are not advocating that you watch the shows every day and all day. Just look at a few of them during your free time. From television courts, you will learn such things as the following:

- Do not lend money to family and friends. If you do, get a written contract. Judge Marilyn Milian often says on her show, *The People's Court*, to use toilet paper if you have to; just write it down.
- Do not give or lend money to your boyfriend. Afterward, you may never see him again.
- Do not cosign a note for someone unless you are able and willing to pay the balance.
- Do not share a cellular telephone service.
- Do not purchase things in your name for someone else (such as a car, apartment, house, utilities, furniture, and whatever else someone can ask).
- Do not have work done at your home or office without a contract with full details. This includes work on your car,

air conditioner, refrigerator, and other valuable equipment
you have.

- Do not pay money without getting a receipt. You need the
receipt to prove payment.

These are just a few of the lessons to learn. Just about every
episode, someone is suing someone for the above common issues.
Let it stop with you. These cases show the best ways to lose a
relationship with family or friends. Sometimes, they may get angry
with you, if you do not do what they want. My father said, and I
believed him: "It is better for them to be angry with you than you
being angry with them and yourself for doing it." Is that deep or
what? It will cost you in the long run.

The only traditional court shows still remaining on the air from
the 1990s or earlier are *The People's Court* (1981), *Judge Judy* (1996),
and *Judge Mathis* (1999). Here is a list of some of the popular court
shows on television at this time:

- *Judge Judy*
- *Judge Mathis*
- *Justice for All with Judge Cristina Perez*
- Judge Jeanine Pirro
- *Judge Karen's Court* (Karen Mills-Francis)
- *Judge Rinder* (ITV, ITV Studios, 2014–present): an hour-long
British reality court show that has aired since August 11, 2014
- *Hot Bench*
- Judge Faith Jenkins
- *Divorce Court*
- *Paternity Court*
- *The People's Court* with Judge Marilyn Milian
- *America's Court* with Judge Ross

There are valuable topics covered in many of the talk shows
on television and radio. Yes, there are some on the internet. Some
of these discussions are led by professionally trained people or
have professionally trained guests. Some are led by people who

are attempting to offer common sense advice. At any rate, you can learn about common problems and how you rank in the midst. You may be able to get some useful information. Many of these shows offer references and established resources to help with many of the problems discussed on the show.

There are too many talk shows to list. There are several that we have enjoyed over the years. You have several hundreds of shows out there from which you can pick. These are the ones that we have enjoyed in the past:

- Anderson Cooper, *Anderson Cooper 360*
- Ellen Degeneres, *The Ellen DeGeneres Show*
- Whoopi Goldberg, *The View*
- Steve Harvey, *Steve Harvey* (TV series)
- Gayle King, co-anchor of *CBS This Morning* and an editor-at-large for *O, The Oprah Magazine*
- Rachel Maddow, *The Rachel Maddow Show* (MSNBC)
- Dr. Phil McGraw, *Dr. Phil*
- Sheryl Underwood, *The Talk*

There is a diversified group of hosts that cover a wide range of topics. You can learn something from each of them. Choose those that address your topic of interest. Some of the talk shows address interesting hobbies, teach skills, and offer tips on health and fitness.

Books

Books, next to the internet, are the fastest method to learn new things. Just about every topic is addressed in a book. Self-help books are top sellers. A "self-help book is one that is written with the intention to instruct its readers on solving personal problems" (https://en.wikipedia.org/ wiki/Self-help_book). According to a Market Data Enterprises market report, the US self-improvement market is worth $9.6 billion (http://answers.google.com/ answers/ threadview/id/786161.html). You can learn just about any subject in the privacy of your home. Books can be purchased at local bookstores, college or university bookstores, large bookstore chains, and online bookstores. Review the preface for a list of recommended options.

There are two books by Steve Harvey that have led to many fiery discussions about women dealing with men. This writer loved the books and wished these books had been available during her early years of dating. Some people disagree with his major points. This writer believes that everybody should at least read them and see how these suggestions can impact their lives. These are the books written by Steve Harvey:

- *Act Like a Lady, Think Like a Man*
- *Straight Talk, No Chaser: How to Find, Keep, and Understand a Man*

Search any of the book websites to select a book. You can read about the authors and reviews of each book to help you to choose a book to help yourself learn something new on a given topic.

Workshops, Seminars, and Conferences

The city where you live can have many options. Some churches offer workshops, seminars, and conferences on many topics including finance, taxes, relationships, faith, health, marriage and family, and many others. Many organizations and businesses in the community offer these services related to their specialties, such as coping with problem children, violence in the home, divorce, and others. Also, local colleges and universities offer courses, workshops, seminars, conferences, and a wide range of other events that can meet your needs. These are often offered free or a small fee. These are usually announced in the local newspaper, on television, on radio and on the internet. Another option is a large-scale workshop, seminar, or conference. These are often sponsored by mega-churches or ministries, companies specializing in conducting these services, and others. These are not usually free. The prices may vary depending on the sponsors. These are usually published in magazines, on the internet, on television, and on radio. Any of these can range from a single day to a weekend or a several-day event. You can choose the one that best fits your interests, needs, and/or budget.

Recommended Resources

To help you get started in your search for helpers, the following resources are recommended:

Internet Search

- http://www.assessment.com/?Accnum=06-5639-106.00
- http://www.forbes.com/forbes/welcome/
- http://www.lifehack.org/articles/work/how-find-career-mentors-more-easily.html
- http://www.usnews.com/education/best-colleges/articles/2013/09/16/find-a-career-mentor-in-college
- http://www.careercast.com/career-news/finding-right-professional-mentor

Books

- Biehl, B. (2005). *Mentoring: How to find a mentor and how to become one.* Aylen Publishing.
- Druce, E. (2015). *This is where to start: Find superstar mentors, master all they know, and get ahead in your career.* Amazon Digital Services, Inc.
- Hewlett, S. A. (2013). *Forget a mentor, find a sponsor: The new way to fast-track your career.* Harvard Business Review Press.
- Kostucki, N., & Chen, L. (2014). *Seek to keep: How to find the best mentors and keep them.* Amazon Digital Services, Inc.
- Mullally, J., & Trimborn, E. (2012). *Business mentoring success secrets: How to find and work with top professional mentors to boost your business. 1ˢᵗ ed.* Eternal Spiral Books. Retrieved from http:// EternalSpiralBooks.com

Books on Child-Rearing

There are many books on this topic. You can choose based on the type of books you love. In fact, bookstores have a large section on this topic. Here are some suggestions:

- American Academy of Pediatrics. (2009). *Caring for your baby and young children, 5th ed.* Publishers: Bantam.
- Bigner, J. J. (2015). *Parent-child relations: An introduction to parenting, 9th ed.* Publisher: Pearson.
- Cline, F., & Fay, J. (2006). *Parenting with love and logic.* Publisher: NavPress.
- Durban, K. G. (2012). *Parenting with Scripture: A Topical Guide for Teachable Moments.* Publisher: Moody.
- Fitzpatrick, E. M., & Thompson, J. (2011). *Give them grace: Dazzling your kids with the love of Jesus.* Publisher: Crossway.
- Hearron, P. L., & Hiblebrand, V. P. (2012). *Guiding young children, 9th ed.* Publisher: Pearson.
- Heath, P. (2012). *Parent-child relations: Context, research, and application, 3rd ed.* Publisher: Pearson.
- MacArthur, J. F. (2000). *What the Bible says about parenting: Biblical principles for raising godly children.* Publisher: Thomas Nelson.
- Markham, L. (2012). *Peaceful parent, happy kids: How to stop yelling and start connecting.* Publisher: Perigee Books.
- Spock, B., & Needlman, R. (2011). *Dr. Spock's baby and child care, 9th ed.* Publisher: Pocket Books.

Personal Notes from the Author

I was fortunate to have parents who were good teachers on most topics. Their methods were not the best. They were dictators, and the punishment for failing to follow the rules was pretty harsh. However, I learned the lessons. I learned my role as a female and how to be respected as a "good girl" and "good citizen." I did not learn about the dynamics of man-and-woman relationships very well. They spent a lot of energy on discouraging these relationships while I was in high school. They were very strict and discouraged every boyfriend-girlfriend interaction. We were not allowed to have a boyfriend before age eighteen. That is a different story. During my day, parents were extremely fearful of teenage pregnancy. You can really understand this, since girls at that time were kicked out of school and church, and even lost their jobs, if they were not married. It was definitely important for mothers to teach their daughters the truth and consequences of sex. Also, during my time, birth control was not fully implemented as we know it today. As a result, important topics about realistic expectations about a relationship were covered in those terms. Therefore, the girls were taught about housekeeping, cooking, managing money, caring for children, respecting adults, spirituality, and getting a good education. You were expected to grow up and become a wife and mother. You got an education should you become divorced or widowed. These good lessons did help me later in life. I give my parents 100 percent credit, since I have become both.

As a single parent, I know how difficult it is. You have no one to share the responsibilities of parenting. I was unfortunate in that I did not have adequate support from family and friends. However, there were times that I had a couple of people who would help in emergency situations. I am eternally grateful for them. If you have support from family and friends, you are tremendously blessed. Take a few moments to express your appreciation to your family and to those special friends. Do not forget to give God the praise for them.

Not only do you have to balance job and home, but you also have to deal with deadbeat fathers (not all men, but too many), child care when you are at work, the schools, homework, and the list goes on. As a result, you do not have time for yourself.

I was unable to afford child care when I was not working. To pay for child care for social outings would be beyond my budget. I had to build my social life around child-friendly activities: Eating in restaurants on the nights that children under a certain age ate free, attending church activities, and socializing with family and friends. I was able to attend my monthly sorority meetings. The sorority sisters loved my children and were looking forward to seeing my children. I had to leave organizations that did not appreciate my bringing my children to meetings. They could not see that I had a lot to give. It was their loss. I decided not to attend any other events where children were not allowed. I recommend that you try to become friends with people who have children around your children's age. To meet this need, many churches, schools, and community organizations offer a program known as "mothers' night out."

In my case, I was an older woman when I began having children. I had gotten an early start in completing my education and establishing my career. If you are in this situation, I want you to know that you are not alone. It is still not too late to make changes in your life. Your children will be your greatest supports. I know this personally. When I changed careers by attending nursing school and graduate school in nursing, my children were great. They gave me their permission and support by helping me with housekeeping chores, making sacrifices for the common goals, and showing their willingness to see their mother succeed. Can you believe that at young ages, they helped me with parts of the housework and school assignments? They were practice subjects for assessment classes, they went with me to the library, and they helped me with doing my library activities, such as locating books and copying materials. I will be eternally grateful to them. Often, your children are your best support. Note that you may be lucky enough to be able to depend on your husband or boyfriend to help you. In fact, many times, these individuals will try to block your academic efforts by making them difficult. Do not be surprised that your man could become intimidated, fearful, and threatened by the changes you are making in your life toward improvement and advancement.

Just remember, your children will grow up. It may seem like a long time. I know that God will help you through this challenge and give you the strength that you need. Remember that children are a blessing and will give you a legacy that will live on forever.

CHAPTER 2

Getting Smart about Your Self-Worth

We all have dreams. But in order to
make dreams come into reality, it
takes an awful lot of determination,
dedication, self-discipline, and effort.

—Jesse Owens

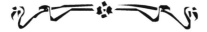

The way you see yourself determines your behavior, attitude, and emotions. It also determines your success in life. When you believe that you are worthy of the good things of life, you are willing to receive these things, work for these things, and be happy with your accomplishments and achievements. The opposite is true. If you do not believe that you are worthy of the good things of life, you are not willing to accept and receive these things. You do not believe that you can succeed. You believe that other people deserve these more than you do. We are talking about your self-worth.

The dictionary defines self-worth as "the sense of one's own value or worth as a person" (http://www.psychalive.org/self-worth/). Dr. Margaret Paul (2006) proposed several questions to determine how you define your self-worth. For example, these are several of questions she recommends for you to ask yourself to help you define your self-worth (http://www.innerbonding. com/show-article/228/defining-self-worth.html):

- "Do you define your worth externally, through others' approval of your looks and performance?"
- "Does your weight, your hair, your money, your job, your car, your clothes, your house, your mate, or the people you know define your worth?"

These questions set the stage for understanding what Dr. Paul calls a "wounded self." According to her, "the wounded self is the part of us that is externally defined. When we are operating from our wounded self, we are constantly trying to look right and perform right, in order to get others to like us, love us, or approve of us. The wounded part of us feels worthy only when receiving validation from others."

According to Dr. Paul, this creates much anxiety. She further states that we feel unsafe when our whole sense of worth hinges upon having control over getting others' approval. We may even feel panicked when we fear making mistakes and running the risk of disapproval and rejection. We may find ourselves judging ourselves in our effort to get ourselves to look "right" or do things "right."

Sherry Collier (n.d.) offered five practical tips to build your self-worth so that you can value yourself while also valuing others (http://creativepathtogrowth.com/self-worth-versus-self-esteem/).

1. "Know This and Own This: Intrinsic value comes from the fact that you were 'fearfully and wonderfully made' by your Creator (Psalm 139:14)."

Collier believes that God exists outside of time and space (God created time and space); therefore, He knew you and designed you before you were even born. So, my question to you is: Why do we try to change what God has created in us?

2. "Discover and Recognize: Actively set out to discover your unique personality traits, skills, gifts, talents, weaknesses, and passions/interests. The more you become acquainted with your unique self, the more you will come to see that there is only one you."

3. "Nourish and Build: Nurture your mindset and your beliefs by feeding your mind positive, uplifting thoughts. Turn away from negative, self-critical, and other-critical thoughts." She specifically recommended that we should read materials that builds us up, listen to music that enriches and uplifts us, fill our eyes with beautiful colors, shapes, and textures and read other Scriptures about how God has a love-story to tell you (God is in love with us, because we are, after all, the Creator's masterpieces).

4. "Act." The next step Collier recommends is for us to put the knowledge and skills gained from the previous steps into action. These knowledge and skills will help us to make the changes that we need to make to change the directions of our lives. When we know or learn better, we should act better. Collier further stated that "One way to start acting on your personal value is to put your unique gifts to use— help others, enrich the world, build up other people so they can also know their own value."

5. "Keep Returning: to truth." She gives an important warning: "Don't let marketing and advertising lead you back down the path of thinking you must look a certain way, smell a certain way, or hang out with certain people to be accepted. Accept yourself unconditionally, faults, foibles, and *all!* Look out your eyes at all the other people around you and find

the preciousness in them as well. The more you keep reminding yourself of your worth and others' worth— the more you will strengthen your self-concept."

Here are some books that can help you with your journey:

- Anthony, R. (2008). *The ultimate secrets to total self-confidence* (Rev.). Berkley Publisher.
- Brown, B. (2010). *The gifts of imperfection: Let go of who you think you're supposed to be and embrace who you are.* Hazeldon Publisher.
- Curtis, J. L., & Cornell, L. (2007). *I'm gonna like me: Letting off a little self-esteem.* HarperCollins Publisher.
- Davis, M. (2008). *The relaxation and stress reduction workbook* (New Harbinger Self-Help Workbook series). New Harbinger Publishers.
- Horn, S. (2000). *What's holding you back? 30 days to having the courage and confidence to do what you want, meet whom you want, and go where you want.* New York: St. Martin's Griffin.
- McKay, M., & Fanning, P. (2005). *The self-esteem companion: Simple exercises to help you challenge your inner critic and celebrate your personal strength.* New Harbinger Publisher.
- McKay, M., & Sutker, C. (2005). *The self-esteem guided journal: A 10-week program* (New Harbinger Guided Journal series). Oakland, CA: New Harbinger.
- Sorensen, M. (2006). *Breaking the chain of low self-esteem.* Prescott, AZ: Wolf Publishing.
- Sutker, C., & McKay, M. (2012). *Self-esteem companion* (2nd ed.). RealHowYouWant Publisher.

Here are some suggested websites to also help with your self-esteem and self-worth building journey:

- Self-esteem tips: http://www.spiritwire.com/selfesteemtips. html

- http://store.samhsa.gov/shin/content/SMA-3715/SMA-3715.pdf
- The difference between self-esteem and self-confidence: http://www.healthyplace.com/blogs/buildingselfesteem/2012/05/the-difference-between-self-esteem-and-self-confidence/
- Self-Worth versus self-esteem:
- http://brendastanton.com/self-worth-vs-self-esteem
- Self-Worth: http://www.hawaii.edu/intlrel/LTPA/selfwort.htm
- Self- Worth and building self-esteem: http://www.healthyplace.com/blogs/buildingselfesteem/2014/10/self-worth-and-building-self-esteem/
- Self- help and self-development: http://www. self-help-and-self-development.com/self-esteem-affirmations.html
- http://www.huffingtonpost.ca/2013/02/07/boost-your-self-esteem_n_2632824.html

Making a Change

Another strategy that is difficult for some people involves making major changes in their lives. Change is essential to your growth and development. People do not like change. However, there comes a time when we must step up to change. Like all of us, you have surely encountered negative people who are not supportive and who try to belittle you. They may disagree with your goals or offer reasons why you cannot achieve your goals. They may make fun of your efforts. They tell you that you are not worthy of your goal. You have to eliminate these people from your life. You cannot seek advice from them. You have to find people who are motivating, supportive, and busy achieving and accomplishing goals for themselves. Find people who are good mentors and models, and who are successful in your endeavors to be the center of your attention.

You have to change your hang-out places. People who are doing the same things hang out together. They do not welcome outsiders. To be successful, go where successful people hang out. These places may include churches, libraries, workshops, seminars, conferences, sporting events, and community events. You many join an organization that focuses on your area of interest, hobbies, beliefs, or discipline.

Finally, make a decision to identify with a higher power; this is so very important. There are things that we can change, and there are many, many things that we cannot change. We have to learn to cope with these. Graham V. Ledgewood (2001) stated that faith is a very powerful means for fulfillment. He further stated that if "you live in faith, you not only have greater momentum toward your goal, you not only streamline your life and you are relieved of many inner conflicts. Also, some amazing transformations in your daily life or career often happen. This is why faith is so greatly encouraged, even in those who are by nature extremely skeptical" (http://www.themystic. org/index.htm).

Having a higher power is part of a number of programs to change negative behavior. It is an essential part of most twelve-step programs. In most twelve-step programs, a higher power can be defined as anything that one believes is one's higher power; in other words, a higher power is determined by the individual. Reported examples of higher powers include nature, consciousness, existential freedom, God, science, and Buddha. There is basically one qualification for identifying a higher power. It is frequently stipulated that as long as a higher power is "greater" than the individual, then the only condition is that it should also be loving and caring (https://en.wikipedia.org/wiki/ Higher_Power).

Researchers have discovered that people with religious beliefs tend to be more content in life and healthier (http://www. dailygalaxy.com/ my_weblog/2009/08/does-religion-make-people-happier-scientists-search-to-explain-why-people-believe-in-a-god. html). For example, Idler (2008) studied this topic extensively. She found that there are many positive benefits that religious and spiritual practices can have on one's health and wellbeing. She also found that starting at an early age, the choices that one makes are based on spiritual beliefs and values directly related to the creation of certain lifestyle habits, such as diet, alcohol use, and sexual practices. Additionally, Idler (2008) found that the benefit of a religious community made up of a variety of individuals from many generations also provides a strong sense of support and connection. She concluded that the overall effect of such practices on one's health and wellbeing is found to be positive throughout one's lifetime (http://spirituality.ucla.edu/docs/ newsletters/4/Idler_ Final.pdf).

Stephanie Pappas (2012) also investigated the benefits of religious involvement. She identified "Eight Ways Religion Impacts Your Life" (http:// www.livescience.com/18421-religion-impacts-health. html). According to Pappas, "many people adhere to religion for the sake of their souls, but it turns out that regular participation in faith-based activities is good for the body and mind, too." Here are some of the ways she found that religion can make people happier and healthier:

- "Helps you resist junk food"
- "Puts a smile on your face"
- "Raises self-esteem (if you live in the right place)"
- "Soothes anxiety"
- "Protects against depressive symptoms"
- "Motivates doctor visits"
- "Lowers your blood pressure"
- "Could make you fat"

The last benefit may not be a positive one. Pappas wrote that "according to a study presented at an American Heart Association meeting in March 2011, young adults who frequently attend religious activities are 50 percent more likely to be obese by middle age than those who stay away from church. It is believed that the culprit is likely Sunday potlucks and other comfort foods associated with worship, according to the researchers. However, the study should not be taken to represent overall health. Religious people tend to live longer than the non-religious, in part because they smoke less." I can image that smoking, using drugs and other risky behaviors are also less frequent among religious individuals.

Pappas concluded that "the benefits seem pegged to how faithful believers are in their church routines." Pappas further found that people who "went once a month or less often had a half-point blood pressure benefit over non-attendees, and people who went between one and three times a month had a one-point reduction in blood pressure. This difference may be due to the fact that the faithful may get lessons in coping with stress and anxiety from the pulpit, according to the researchers cited in the studies, or they might get a relaxation boost by singing, praying and performing rituals with others." It will definitely help with a good diet and exercise regime.

Personal Notes from the Author

Religion has been an important component of my life. My co-members of my church are positive and helpful in building the members' self-esteem. My religious faith gives me a reason not to worry and become anxious about the matters of life. It gives me strength to face the unexpected events that we often face from day to day. There is a strong support system that comes with being a member of a congregation of similar-minded people. These similar-minded people give the motivation, love, caring, and encouragement that we need to achieve our God-given talents. Plus, my church offers all kinds of activities designed to help us as a group to learn and grow toward being more informed, skilled, compassionate, caring, loving, helpful, sharing, and assisting us to be overall better persons.

We have the freedom of choice. It is my perspective that you could not go wrong with choosing God as your higher power. It is important to have faith in something greater than yourself. Otherwise, you would turn to unhealthy activities to deal with the stress and problems of life. This is part of the reason why people seek comfort in drinking alcohol, drugs, gambling, and other addictive activities.

CHAPTER 3

Getting Smart about Men

Boys love you because they need you.
Men need you because they love you.

—Unknown Author

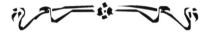

The way some women think about men poses a challenge for most women. From a very young age, most girls are taught that their mission in life is to get a husband and children. However, they were not taught about the rules of the game. Many are left to find their own means of achieving the goal. This has resulted in disappointment for many girls and women.

The rate of divorce in America is high; it has been reported by various organizations that the rate of divorce is 50 percent (http://www. ivorcestatistics.info/divorce-statistics-and-divorce-rate-in-the-usa.html). Most divorces are filed by women. It is believed that a generation ago, women were less likely to file for divorce even if they were in unhappy or abusive marriages. This is due to the fact that most were financially dependent on their spouses and others feared the social stigma of divorce.

According to an article written by Cathy Meyer (2015), a divorce expert, there are several reasons that women are filing for divorce (http://www.divorcestatistics.info/divorce-statistics-and-divorce-rate-in-the-usa.html). These reasons include the following:

- Women filed for divorce to get "relief from a bad marriage." Women no longer believe that they have to be married in order to be happy. If their needs are not being met, they want to leave the marriage.
- Women filed divorce to "escape domestic abuse." In reference to this point, another organization offers some important data. According to the 2015 Domestic Violence Statistics (http://domesticviolencestatistics. org/domestic-violence-statistics/):
  - o "Every nine seconds in the US a woman is assaulted or beaten."
  - o "Around the world, at least one in every three women has been beaten, coerced into sex or otherwise abused during her lifetime. Most often, the abuser is a member of her own family."
  - o "Domestic violence is the leading cause of injury to women—more than car accidents, muggings, and rapes combined."
  - o "Studies suggest that up to ten million children witness some form of domestic violence annually."
  - o "Nearly one in five teenage girls who have been in a relationship said a boyfriend threatened violence or self-harm if presented with a breakup."
  - o "Every day in the US, more than three women are murdered by their husbands or boyfriends."

These statistics show us that there is a lot of work needed to protect women and their children. It begins with proper education of our girls and women.

Looking back at Meyer (2015), the reasons for divorce include these additional reasons:

- "Fewer women are financially dependent on a husband" (http://www.divorcestatistics. info/divorce-statistics-and-divorce-rate-in-the-usa.html). Women are educated and working at careers that help them to be more financially independent. Therefore, they are less likely to tolerate many things in marriage.

- "Women are less tolerant of infidelity." Women have placed a high value on their worth and believe that they have something to offer in a marriage. As a result, they have higher expectations.
- "Women want more out of marriage." Women are no longer looking for someone to take care of them. They want more, which includes a strong positive relationship, a good companion, and a lifetime partner.
- "Women lose their identity." Women no longer want their identity primarily tied to being wives and mothers. They love being wives and mothers. However, they have more to offer, and they work hard to take on other roles in society and the world. They want credit for these achievements.

Meyer concluded that the one thing most women who divorce have in common is a new sense of empowerment. She further wrote that women view themselves as equal to men. In some marriages, this does not happen, and these marriages take away a sense of equality instead of promoting feelings of equality. Women have and should continue to work hard for the advancement of women. They will not allow marriage, especially a bad one, to take this away these opportunities from them.

Parents must take the lead in teaching their children about healthy relationships. The best form of teaching is imitation. Parents who live in a healthy relationship demonstrate how this is done. Whether parents are in a good or bad relationship, parents must take time to talk to their children. An article entitled "Talk with Your Teen about Healthy Relationships" is a must-read for parents. According to the author, talking about healthy relationships is a great way to show that parents are available to listen and answer questions; the author encourages parents to make sure to check in often with their teens (http://healthfinder.gov/ HealthTopics/ Category/parenting/healthy-communication-and-relationships/ talk-with-your-teen-about-healthy-relationships). The author further recommends that parents should agree on clear rules about dating to help keep the teen safe.

The author of the article shared some interesting statistics. More than one in ten teens who has been on a date has also experienced one of the following:

- Being physically abused (hit, pushed, or slapped) by someone they have gone out with
- Being sexually abused (kissed, touched, or forced to have sex without wanting to) by someone they have dated

The author of this article believes that parents can help their kids to obtain the following skills:

- "Develop skills for healthy and safe relationships"
- "Set expectations for how they want to be treated"
- "Recognize when a relationship is unhealthy"

Some of the essential topics recommended that should be included in your talk with your children:

- "What makes a relationship healthy?"

  According to the article, a healthy relationship has these characteristics:
  o "Both people feel respected, supported, and valued."
  o "Both partners make decisions together."
  o "Both people have friends and interests outside of the relationship."
  o "The couple settles disagreements with open and honest communication."
  o "There are more good times than bad."

- "What makes a relationship unhealthy?"
  According to the article, an unhealthy relationship has these characteristics:

- o "One person tries to change the other."
- o "One person makes most or all of the decisions."
- o "One or both people drop friends and interests outside of the relationship."
- o "One or both people yell, threaten, hit, or throw things during arguments."
- o "One person makes fun of the other's opinions or interests."
- o "One person keeps track of the other all the time by calling, texting, or checking in with friends."
- o "There are more bad times than good."

- "What is dating violence?"
  According to the article, dating violence occurs "when one person in a romantic relationship is abusive to the other person." This includes the following behaviors:
  - o Stalking
  - o Emotional, physical, and sexual abuse

Who is at risk for dating violence?

According to the same article, teens who are at risk of being in unhealthy relationships have the following problems:

- Use alcohol or drugs
- Are depressed
- Hang out with friends who are violent
- Have trouble controlling their anger
- Struggle with learning in school
- Have sex with more than one person
- Have experienced violence at home or in the community

What are the warning signs of dating violence?

Sudden changes in a teen's attitude or behavior could mean that something more serious is going on. A conversation with the teen is very important to determine what is going on.

Watch for signs that your teen's partner may be violent.

The possible signs that a teen is in a relationship with someone who uses violence may include the following:

- Avoiding friends, family, and school activities
- Making excuses for a partner's behavior
- Looking uncomfortable or fearful around a partner
- Losing interest in favorite activities
- Getting lower grades in school
- Having unexplained injuries, like bruises or scratches

These are just some of the topics covered in this article. Please read the full article for a fuller understanding on how to address the topic.

Recommended Resources

To get you started in your search for a mate, there is some basic knowledge that we must obtain. We must be able to learn from other people's mistakes and from professionals, such as marriage and family counselors, ministers, psychologists, and psychotherapists.

Internet Search
- http://www.wikihow.com/Find-the-Ideal-Mate
- http://marriagemissions.com/what-should-you-look-for-in-a-mate/
- http://resources.grantedministries.org/article/qualities_for_potential_mate_d_e.pdf

- http://bibleresources.org/christian-marriage-choosing
  -a-mate/
- http://www.globalchristians.org/articles/findwife.htm
- http://thoughtcatalog.com/brian-n-gates/2014/01/18-
  qualities-you-need-to-find-in-a-partner-before-you-
  commit-to-them/
- http://elitedaily.com/dating/the-one-10-traits-your-ideal-
  soul-mate-should-have/
- http://www.beliefnet.com/Love-Family/Relationships
  /2009/01/Find-Your-Soul-Mate.aspx

Books

- Billingsley, R.T. (2011). *A good man is hard to find.* Gallery
  Books Publisher.
- Grace, S. (2015). *Eight Quick and Easy Tips to Attract
  Men: How to Get the Guy You Want.* Amazon Digital
  Services, Inc.
- Harvey, S. (2009). *Act Like a Lady, Think Like a Man: What
  Men Really Think About Love, Relationships, Intimacy, and
  Commitment.* Amistad Publisher.
- Harvey, S. (2012). *Straight Talk, No Chaser: How to Find,
  Keep, and Understand a Man.* Amistad Publisher.
- Hussey, M. (2014). *Get the Guy: Learn Secrets of the Male
  Mind to Find the Man You Want and the Love You Deserve.*
  Harper Wave Publisher.
- McDowell, B., & Attract Love. (2013). *Love: How to Find
  Love. Attract the Man or Woman of Your Dreams, Find
  Love. Be Happy with Your Soulmate.* Amazon Digital
  Services, Inc.
- O'Conner, F. (1977). *A Good Man Is Hard to Find and
  Other Stories.* Harvest/Hbj Book. (A classic.)

Biblical Love

The Bible contains some of the best love stories known to man. By reading these stories, we can learn what love should or should not look like. Here is a list of the most famous Bible couples:

- Adam and Eve (Genesis 2–3)
- Abraham and Sarah (Genesis 15–17)
- Jacob and Rachel (Genesis 29)
- Ruth and Boaz (Ruth 1–4)
- The bride and groom in the Song of Solomon
- Mary and Joseph (Matthew 1)
- Isaac and Rebekah (Genesis 24)
- Jacob, Rachel, and Leah (the love story in Genesis 20)
- Michal and David (1 Samuel 18–19)
- David and Bathsheba (2 Samuel 11–12)
- Samson and Delilah (Judges 16)

Then, there are Bible verses that can help us to understand the meaning of true love in general and in a relationship. A few of these are listed below:

- 1 Corinthians 13:4–7
- 1 Corinthians 13:13
- 1 John 4:7
- Romans 13:10
- John 15:13
- Romans 13:8–10
- 1 John 4:11
- 1 Peter 4:8
- 1 John 3:16–18
- Mark 12:31
- 1 Corinthians 16:14

Personal Notes from the Author

As I study the life of Jesus and the Bible, I have learned that if a person does not know Jesus and God, he or she does not know the meaning of true love. Without the knowledge of the meaning of true love, one does not really know how to love oneself. If one does know how to love oneself, how can one love another person? When I look back at the men in my life, I find that those who had self-love, self-esteem, and self-worth issues were unable to give mature, biblical love. They were selfish, self-centered, uncaring, and immature in their thinking and behaving.

I am totally convinced that these men did not love themselves, which resulted in them being unable to give and receive love. See, if you feel good about yourself, you will treat others as you wish to be treated. When you believe that you deserve love, can be trusted, can be faithful, and most of all, are able to give love, then you will feel complete and mature, and you will have the ability to give and receive love. To bring this down to earth, an unfaithful, lying, deceitful, demanding, violent man does not have the capability to love you. I say run and run fast from him. You will get over him. It is better to know what you are dealing with and leave rather than to hurt indefinitely suffering through the inevitable. You have to be strong for yourself, your children, and other people in your life. It will take prayers, meditation, and keeping yourself busy with positive activities that enhance your self-esteem and self-worth.

If you learn nothing else from this book, you must learn that true love does not hurt. It does not bring physical or emotional pain. True love comes to build and restore. It compliments you. It respects you as a person and as a woman. All words and actions should add to building and restoring you as a person. Any word that belittles should be a hint to get out. Any physical encounter is a hint to run and to run very fast. Do not delay to leave, even if you have to leave with the clothes on your back. You can always get new and different stuff. Your life is precious. If it is taken, you cannot get another one.

There are a number of resources available for women in situations of domestic violence. These include:

- The National Domestic Violence Hotline 1- 800-799-7233 1-800-787-3224 (TTY) http://www.thehotline.org/
- HelpGuide.org http://www.helpguide.org/articles/abuse/ help-for-abused-and-battered-women.htm
- U.S. Department of Health and Human Services http:// www.acf.hhs.gov/programs/fysb/resource/help-fv

US State and Territorial Coalitions

The National Network to End Domestic Violence (NNEDV) represents the fifty-six US state and territorial coalitions against domestic violence. Domestic violence coalitions serve as state-wide and territory-wide leaders in the effort to end domestic violence. These organizations connect local domestic violence service providers and are valuable resources for information about services, programs, legislation, and policies that support survivors of domestic violence (http://nnedv.org/ resources/coalitions.html).

If you are in danger, this organization recommends that you immediately call 911, the US. National Domestic Violence Hotline at 1-800-799-7233, or your local/state hotline. Here is a list of this network by state:

- Alabama Coalition Against Domestic Violence
- Alaska Network on Domestic Violence and Sexual Assault
- American Samoa Alliance Against Domestic and Sexual Violence
- Arizona Coalition Against Domestic Violence
- Arkansas Coalition Against Domestic Violence
- California Partnership to End Domestic Violence
- Colorado Coalition Against Domestic Violence
- Connecticut Coalition Against Domestic Violence
- Delaware Coalition Against Domestic Violence
- DC Coalition Against Domestic Violence
- Florida Coalition Against Domestic Violence
- Georgia Coalition Against Domestic Violence
- Guam Coalition Against Sexual Assault and Family Violence

- Hawaii State Coalition Against Domestic Violence
- Idaho Coalition Against Sexual and Domestic Violence
- Illinois Coalition Against Domestic Violence
- Indiana Coalition Against Domestic Violence
- Iowa Coalition Against Domestic Violence
- Kansas Coalition Against Sexual and Domestic Violence
- Kentucky Domestic Violence Association
- Louisiana Coalition Against Domestic Violence
- Maine Coalition to End Domestic Violence
- Maryland Network Against Domestic Violence
- Massachusetts Coalition Against Sexual Assault and Domestic Violence
- Michigan Coalition to End Domestic and Sexual Violence
- Minnesota Coalition for Battered Women
- Mississippi Coalition Against Domestic Violence
- Missouri Coalition Against Domestic and Sexual Violence
- Montana Coalition Against Domestic and Sexual Violence
- Nebraska Domestic Violence Sexual Assault Coalition
- Nevada Network Against Domestic Violence
- New Hampshire Coalition Against Domestic and Sexual Violence
- New Jersey Coalition for Battered Women
- New Mexico Coalition Against Domestic Violence
- New York State Coalition Against Domestic Violence
- North Carolina Coalition Against Domestic Violence
- CAWS North Dakota
- Northern Marianas Coalition Against Domestic and Sexual Violence
- Ohio Domestic Violence Network
- Oklahoma Coalition Against Domestic Violence and Sexual Assault
- Oregon Coalition Against Domestic and Sexual Violence
- Pennsylvania Coalition Against Domestic Violence
- (Puerto Rico) Coordinadora Paz para la Mujer
- Rhode Island Coalition Against Domestic Violence

- South Carolina Coalition Against Domestic Violence and Sexual Assault
- South Dakota Coalition Ending Domestic and Sexual Violence
- Tennessee Coalition Against Domestic and Sexual Violence
- Texas Council on Family Violence
- Utah Domestic Violence Council
- Vermont Network Against Domestic and Sexual Violence
- Virginia Sexual and Domestic Violence Action Alliance
- Virgin Islands Domestic Violence and Sexual Abuse Council
- Washington State Coalition Against Domestic Violence
- West Virginia Coalition Against Domestic Violence
- Wisconsin Coalition Against Domestic Violence
- Wyoming Coalition Against Domestic Violence and Sexual Assault

Next, tell someone. Tell family, friends, coworkers, and law enforcement. They can help you find appropriate resources and support. Lastly, you may need these people to help with a legal defense or some form of charges.

Finally, take classes in self-defense, how to secure your home, and other options of protection. You must empower yourself with all the available knowledge and skills to protect yourself and your children. Your children are especially dependent on you.

Personal Notes from the Author

I believe that these are important basic dos and don'ts that parents should teach their children. These include the following:

Dos
- Examine your goals and how a relationship will advance you in meeting your goals.
- Avoid dream-killers. You need people in your life who will support your dreams.

- Establish standards for your life and relationships in your life. If you expect more, you will get more.
- Develop respect for yourself and others.
- Value your uniqueness and worthiness.
- Study and observe healthy relationships. Use this information to guide all future relationships.
- Think with your head and not with your hormones. There can be many problems that can result from thinking with one's hormones: Unwanted pregnancy, sexually transmitted diseases, and unnecessary pain and suffering.
- Become involved in activities that will build your self-esteem. These include developing a hobby, learning new skills, participating in sports, meeting interesting and positive people, and expanding your education.

Don'ts
- Do not tolerate disrespect.
- Do not disrespect others.
- Do not tolerate verbal, physical, and emotional abuse.
- Do not shack with anybody unless you are married. It is not healthy to do the work of a wife without the legal, spiritual, emotional, and moral benefits of being a wife, and the same is true for husbands.

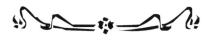

CHAPTER 4

Getting Smart about Your Finances

The starting point of all achievement is
desire. Keep this constantly in mind. Weak
desires bring weak results, just as a small
fire makes a small amount of heat.

—Napoleon Hill, *Think and Grow Rich*

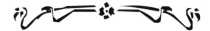

Managing money is a challenging task for a lot of people. It is a serious problem for people who are limited in financial resources. First, you are dependent on other people to manage your business. As a result, your business may be exposed to other people whom you do not want to know your business. Second, you can get into legal problems. Bouncing checks and failing to pay your debts can take you to court. Third, you can get a poor credit rating. This could cause you difficulty in major purchases such as a house, a car, and large appliances. It can impact your getting a job. Also, you may lose your professional license. Finally, the tax guys may come after you.

To become an independent woman, you have to gain control of your finances. There are many sources of financial advice. Parents tend to be the first advisors.

Some of the advice that parents give includes the following tips:

- Do not lend money. The best way to lose a relationship is to lend money. If you cannot afford to give the other person the money, do not lend.
- Do not cosign with anybody on any financial obligation. If the individual does not pay, you are obligated to pay. That can be serious trauma—to end up paying for someone else's car, jewelry, furniture, clothes, vacations, and so on without the benefits of enjoying these items for yourself.
- Do not make charges on your credit card for someone without getting the cash from the person. You will be stuck with the charges or you will definitely end up in a lawsuit.
- Do not make major purchases with anybody except your spouse. Breaking up is a problem when you own property outside of marriage; the courts may not help you.
- Seek the help of a reliable financial advisor. You must be responsible for planning for your life. Plan for your retirement, education of yourself and/or children, investments, vacations, purchase of a home or vehicle, and other important projects you have for yourself. Only the extremely rich have the luxury of purchasing at will, and they need to be careful or they will not be rich any longer.
- Always have proof of payment. You must get a receipt in all transactions and file the receipts. People get amnesia. If you pay with cash, get a receipt. If you pay with a check, indicate payment information on the check.
- Do not give money to a man. A real man does not ask a woman for money, especially if she is not his wife. It is worst for a man to ask a woman with children for money or any favors that put her and her children at financial risk.
- Do not take on the responsibilities of a wife without the legal, moral, and ethical benefits. There are many men out there who will take advantage of you in meeting their selfish needs. They want you to be responsible for taking care of them. It is not to your advantage to pay the household bills or purchase large items for the family, such as a house, a vehicle, and appliances for the home, for him outside of marriage.

The best advice of all is: "Never spend your money before you have earned it." This is a quote from Thomas Jefferson.

The next step requires you to seek professional help. There are several ways that you can achieve this without spending a lot of money. First, many local organizations, including churches, financial planning agencies, and schools, regularly offer classes on budgeting, planning for retirement, financial planning, investment options, getting started in real estate, tax planning, buying insurance, and other relevant topics to the public.

Second, there are magazines and newspapers that focus on informing the reader about financial matters. These magazines can be purchased from online and land-based bookstores. Some of them offer online editions. You can also subscribe to these magazine or newspaper, and you can get them monthly. By the way, there are financial newspapers and magazines that can be purchased at some grocery stores, pharmacies, gas stations, magazine and newspaper stands, and retail department stores.

These are some of the major magazines and newspapers that you can review:

Magazines

- *Forbes*
- *Fortune*
- *Consumer Reports*
- *Kiplinger's Personal Finance*
- *International Living*
- *US Banker*
- *Moneywise*
- *Financial Planning*
- *Moneyfacts*
- *Insurance Networking News*
- *Fund Strategy*
- *National Mortgage News*
- *Corporate Advisors*
- *Employee Benefits*

Newspapers

- *The Wall Street Journal*
- *Financial Times*

Third, you can attend a local college or university. Most colleges and universities have departments that offer majors in finance, accounting, and management. If you do not plan to get a degree in these areas, you can take an introductory course and some of the lower-division courses in these departments, such as tax laws, banking, insurance, and others.

Next, you can seek direct advice from financial planners, certified public accountants, insurance agents, bankers, tax preparers, and others who do business in your area of interest. You can get recommendations from family, friends, coworkers, and fellow church members.

Finally, your internet should be your best friend by now. The internet is the best tool available to all of us for conducting research. You can research by specific questions or topics. There is an almost endless amount of information on the internet. You just have to be careful. Evaluate the writer of the article. Almost anybody can place an article out there. So, check the information by comparing to more reliable sources.

Some people do best when they take control of what and how they learn. There is nothing wrong with being self-taught. So, go for it. Here is a list of resources that can enhance your learning about the world of finance. These resources can help you with your self-study or with more formal avenues for getting educated about finance.

Recommended Resources

Internet Search

- https://mappingyourfuture.org/Money/
- http://managingmymoney.com/

- http://www.goodhousekeeping.com/life/money/advice/a19098/125-tips-to-save-money/
- http://money.usnews.com/money/personal-finance/slideshows/how-to-manage-your-money-in-your-20s
- http://www.boston.com/business/personalfinance/managingyourmoney/
- http://www.consumer.gov/section/managing-your-money
- http://www.wikihow.com/Category:Managing-Your-Money
- http://money.usnews.com/money/blogs/my-money/2012/03/09/simple-steps-to-manage-your-money
- Edward Jones ® Investigations at https://www.edwardjones.com/campaigns/national/extra-mile.html
- Gallant, C. (2015). Four steps to building a profitable portfolio. Retrieved from http://www. investopedia.com/articles/ pf/05/060805.asp
- Kennon, J. (2015). Six secrets to building a profitable portfolio. Retrieved from http:// beginnersinvest.about.com/od/investment-portfolio-basics/a/Six-Secrets-To-Building-A-Successful-Investment-Portfolio.htm
- Financial Planning at http://financialplanningtips.net/
- How to Choose a Financial Planner at http://guides.wsj.com/personal-finance/managing-your-money/how-to-choose-a-financial-planner/
- Financial Planning at http://learnfinancialplanning.com/
- Vohwinkle, J. (2015). Budgeting 101: Everything You Need to Know About Budgeting. Retrieved from http://financialplan.about.com/od/budgetingyourmoney/tp/budgeting-101.htm
- Budgeting: Practical money skills. (2015). Retrieved from http://financialplan.about. com/od/budgetingyourmoney/tp/budgeting-101.htm

Books

- Frey, A. H., & Frey, A. (2012). *Grow your money the smart and easy way.* Publisher: CreateSpace Independent.

- Gitman, L. J., & Joehnk, M. (2013). *Personal financial planning.* Publisher: South Western College.
- Glover, R., & Brown, A. (2015). *Preparing for retirement: A comprehensive guide to financial planning.* Publisher: CreateSpace Independent.
- Kobliner, B. (2009). *Get a financial life: Personal finance in your twenties and thirties.* Publisher: Simon and Schuster.
- Ramsey, D. (2013). *The total money makeover: Classic Edition: A proven plan for financial fitness.* Publisher: Thomas Nelson.
- Richards, C. (2015). *The one-page financial plan: A simple way to be smart about your money.* Publisher: Portfolio.
- Tyson, E. (2012). *Personal finances for dummies.* Publisher: For Dummies.

Personal Notes from the Author

The more you know, the better you will be. You have to recognize that this is one of the areas that can impact the rest of your life. Obviously, this knowledge can help you with your current life. Just remember:

> It's not how much money you make, but how much money you keep, how hard it works for you, and how many generations you keep it for.
>
> —Robert Kiyosaki

If I could "Turn Back the Hand of Time," I would learn as much as I can about money matters, such as these:

- Saving options
- Banking and finance
- Investment options
- Retirement planning
- Owning real estate

- Taxes
- Stock options
- Financial counselors

The Bible commands us to take care of our families. The Scripture says: "But if any provide not for his own, and especially for those of his own house, he hath denied the faith, and is worse than an infidel" (1 Timothy 5:8, King James Version). Also, we are expected to care for grandchildren. The Scripture about this is clear: "A good man leaveth an inheritance to his children's children: and the wealth of the sinner is laid up for the just" (Proverbs 13:22, KJV). As you can easily see, God has given us responsibilities for caring for our children and grandchildren. I am trying to use every piece of knowledge that I have to help me to leave an inheritance for both my children and grandchildren. The premise is that each generation should do better than previous ones. They should not make the same mistakes. Along with providing the needed monies and properties, we have to equip our children and grandchildren with the valuable knowledge and skills to carry on these God-given responsibilities.

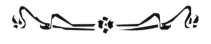

CHAPTER 5

Getting Smart about Your Relationships

Too many people are thinking the grass is greener
on the other side of the fence, when they ought
to just water the grass they are standing on.

—Amar Dave

If you follow the "Golden Rule," most of your relationship issues will be resolved. To put it another way or in a more accurate way, if your significant other would follow the Golden Rule, all of your relationship issues would be resolved. Some of you may have never heard of this rule.

The Golden Rule is the idea that people should treat others in the same way that they themselves would like to be treated. It is often expressed as "Do unto others as you would have them do unto you," which is one translation of a biblical verse, Luke 6:31. Also, this rule is often called the "ethic of reciprocity, variations of this concept can be found in many religions and throughout history. Some versions urge people to love other people or to avoid doing harm to others. In each case, the underlying theme is that one should treat other people with kindness

45

and respect (http://www.wisegeek.org/what-is-the-golden-rule.htm#did youknowout).

This writer believes that if we all lived by this rule, there would be a decrease in the numbers of breakups, physical and verbal abuse, fights, war, conflicts, violence, and crime. Many of these problems that we face in a relationship would simply be eliminated or minimized. If you follow the "Golden Rule," you will not cheat on others, steal from others, kill others, or commit any other painful acts against others. The reason is that you would not do these things to yourself. This is as simple as it can be explained.

Give Respect to Receive Respect

We should especially respect other women. We should set our standards high and live by them. If you do not set a high standard, you will fall short of what God has for you. One way of showing respect to other women is by refusing to date married men and other women's men. This goes back to the Golden Rule. Plus, there is a thing called karma. "It also refers to the spiritual principle of cause and effect where intent and actions of an individual (cause) influence the future of that individual (effect). Good intent and good deed contribute to good karma and future happiness, while bad intent and bad deed contribute to bad karma and future suffering" (https://en.wikipedia. org/ wiki/Karma). As many say, karma is a "b," and you do not want to live what you dished out to others.

Pieces of Good Advice

Avoid intimate relationships with people whom you would not marry. First of all, they may very well block any future possibilities. My mother always said, "If you mess with trash, it will get in your eyes." Do not get me wrong. People are not trash, but some people do have trashy ways, and this can cause you to misunderstand or miss valuable signs that you are in the wrong relationship. You have to keep clear eyes and clear thinking. And, keep your focus on your goal.

You cannot worship a man or other people, and you cannot put your faith in people. People are humans and subject to error. These errors can be devastating, if you have all your faith in those people. People are subject to err by using methods they need to obtain essential needs. In other words, they may use you to meet their personal selfish goals. You can get caught up in a difficult situation.

Never love anybody more than God and yourself. If you do, you will be walking on dangerous ground. You must realize that God will not cause you pain in any aspect of your life. Can you say that about people? You may have been disappointed with girlfriends, boyfriends, husbands, coworkers, family, and people that you know. This does not happen with God and His son Jesus.

The point is that we should be careful how involved we can get. The Bible, the greatest book that has ever been written, gives us some guidelines on what to look for in a friend.

- **Proverbs 18:24, English Standard Version** (ESV): "A man of many companions may come to ruin, but there is a friend who sticks closer than a brother."
- **1 Corinthians 15:33** (ESV): "Do not be deceived: "Bad company ruins good morals.""
- **Proverbs 17:17** (ESV): "A friend loves at all times, and a brother is born for adversity."
- **1 Peter 4:8–10** (ESV): "Above all, keep loving one another earnestly, since love covers a multitude of sins. Show hospitality to one another without grumbling. As each has received a gift, use it to serve one another, as good stewards of God's varied grace."
- **Proverbs 22:24–27** (ESV): "Make no friendship with a man given to anger, nor go with a wrathful man, lest you learn his ways and entangle yourself in a snare. Be not one of those who give pledges, who put up security for debts. If you have nothing with which to pay, why should your bed be taken from under you?"

The greatest message is that we must recognize that an ungodly man or woman does not have the basic tools to be a friend. Knowing God and Jesus will help us to know the true meaning of love and friendship.

Resources

In additional to the Bible, there other references that may help you with building strong positive relationships.

Internet

- Alexander, R. (2012). Ten tips for better karma at work. Retrieved from http://www. lifescript.com/well-being/articles/0/
- Christ, S. (2015). *Ten signs you're in a healthy relationship.* Retrieved from http://www.lifehack.org/articles/communication/tell-your-partner-these-10-things-for-relationship-built-last.html
- Hill, D. (2015). Getting along with family. Retrieved from http://www.selfgrowth. com/articles/getting_along_with_family_0.html
- Robinson, L., Boose, G., Smith, M., & Segal, J. (2015). How to make close friends: Tips on meeting people and building strong friendships. Retrieved from http://www. helpguide. org/articles/relationships/how-to-make-friends.htm
- The Friends and Friendship Web. (2008). Acquaintance or friend: Build close friendship: There is no substitute for a friend. Retrieved from http://www. cyberparent.com/friendship/
- WebMD. (2015). Work it out: Getting along with coworkers. Retrieved from http://www.webmd.com/balance/features/getting-along-with-coworkers
- Williams, A. (2008). Twenty-five ways to build stronger relationships. Retrieved from http://www.lifeoptimizer. org/ 2008/08/29/build-stronger-friendships/

Books

- Boucher, J. J., & Boucher, T. (2015). *Mending broken relationships, building strong ones: Eight ways to love as Jesus loves us.* Publisher: Word Among Us Press.
- Moody, V. (2014). *The people facts: How building great relationships and ending bad ones unlocks your God-given purpose.* Publisher: Thomas Nelson.
- Sobel, A., & Panas, J. (2014). *Power relationships: 26 irrefutable laws for building extraordinary relationships.* Publisher: Wiley.
- Treu, J. (2014). *Social Wealth: How to build extraordinary relationships by transforming in the way we live, love, lead, and Network.* Publisher: Be Extraordinary LLC.

Personal Notes from the Author

I love people. Over the years of personal experience and observing others, I have learned that you must keep proper perspectives when you are dealing with people. God should be first in your life. The Holy Spirit will prompt you when things are getting bad. The Holy Spirit has your back. The Bible tells us whom to marry or with whom to have a relationship. I believe that God wants us to be in a healthy relationship and He does not want us to suffer from domestic violence, any form of abuse, neglect, or belittling treatments.

The Bible teaches us that infidelity is a possible way out of a bad marriage. The Bible also speaks about wisdom. Of course, this refers to our relationship with God in following biblical guidance. I personally believe that God made us to be thinking, problem-solving, and critical-thinking beings. We are above the animals and should behave as such. We can evaluate our situation and should know when we are in a bad relationship and should be able to act appropriately. (Refer to Chapter Ten for dealing with a relationship with a man.)

Plus, God does not expect us to live in this world alone. He wants us to use godly wisdom in dealing with people. We cannot become so involved with people that we lose the best relationship, which is with God. Friends should not interfere with relationships with spouses and with your caring for the family.

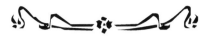

CHAPTER 6

Getting Smart about Your Health

Time and health are two precious assets
that we don't recognize and appreciate
until they have been depleted.

—Denis Waitley

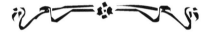

Your health is one of your most valuable assets. We have to learn at an early age and teach our children while they are young to make healthy choices. Old and bad habits are hard to break. Starting out right can keep you grounded in good health.

The Cost of Getting Healthy and Fit

Probably, topics related to health and fitness are the most common topic covered in books, in magazines, and on the internet. Additionally, Americans spend a lot of money on health and fitness. For example, Jae Alexia Lee (n.d.) reviewed data that suggests that "Americans spend between forty and fifty billion dollars annually on weight loss. Many studies suggest that between 60 percent and 90 percent of that is wasted on ineffective dieting where the weight comes back within one to two years" (http://www.quora.com/How-much-money-do-Americans-spend-on-fitness-products-each-year).

Lee also reported that in the health club and gym industry, things are pretty appalling. The author wrote: "The average cost of a gym membership in the United States is $55 per month. The part that gets appalling is that 60 percent or more of gym members never use their membership."

Finally, Lee reported that "Americans spend upwards of thirty billion a year on athletic apparel alone. Designer brands have taken the gym environment as yet another place to showcase fashion. Add the cost of new workout shoes, one or two changes of workout clothes, gym bag, water bottle, etc. to the cost of that January gym membership and once again you have consumers dropping $200 or more on product that they will not use for more than a month." Even the fitness apparel industry is making a lot of money. They also sell products that people will use only a few times.

It is not necessary to spend a lot of money on getting healthy. An essential part of getting healthy and fit is getting a physical checkup and following your health provider's advice. These providers can offer diet plans and suggestions for exercises. Next, independent research studies on health and fitness show that it does not have to be expensive (http://www.quora.com/How-much-money-do-Americans-spend-on-fitness-products-each-year). With a well-thought-out plan, you should choose a couple of books, magazines, and the internet to guide your health and fitness plan. There are so many reference materials out there to list them. Talk with family and friends to get recommendations. If this does not work, try a detailed internet search. You may have developed an interest in some of the well-known athletes, entertainers, and other personalities who have shared their health and fitness secrets. They have often offered the names of their favorite health and fitness experts.

Why Should You Get Healthy and Fit?

The main reasons why people want to get healthy include the following:

- Live longer
- Have a better quality of life

- Feel great
- Be disease-free
- Look good
- Compete in sports
- Have a better appearance on stage, in movies, and on television
- Seek a spouse or a significant other
- Feel good about themselves
- Compete in the business world

Whatever the reason, it is never too late to pursue health and fitness. As stated earlier, it begins with your health provider. Then you continue with studying as much as can about the subject and you will be able to set realistic goals. Prayer and meditation are important parts of a health and fitness plan.

Start with Your Health Provider

Your provider with conduct a complete physical and obtain a comprehensive history. This will help you know your health risk, limitations, and strengths. Any disease processes will be identified and treated, according to current treatment protocols. The treatment protocols may include medications, diet changes, smoking cessation, alcohol and drug counseling, mental health counseling, stress management, relaxation strategies, and others. The provider can offer information about the safety of these for your baseline data for your current health status.

Are Your Goals Realistic?

It is important to set realistic goals. Your health provider may help you with this. Your goals should be based on your age, weight, interest, and what you want to achieve. Your current health status will also impact the goal-setting. Your goal should be research-based. In other words, what do researchers say about the best diets, exercises, supplements, and other health improvement plans for your particular situation?

Getting Rid of Addictions

Addiction is a serious problem for a number of individuals and families. An addiction is recognized as a disease process. Addiction changes the brain in fundamental ways, disturbing a person's normal hierarchy of needs and desires and substituting new priorities connected with procuring and using the drug (http://www. drugabuse.gov/ publications/drugfacts/comorbidity-addiction-other-mental-disorders). The resulting compulsive behaviors that weaken the ability to control impulses, despite the negative consequences, are similar to the hallmarks of other mental illnesses.

Types of Addictions

There are several types of addictions that are recognized by professionals in mental health. The types of addictions are listed so that you recognize that addictions come in many forms. A detailed discussion of each of these is not the intent of this book. Below is a list of recognized addictions.

A list of addictions to substances can be found at http:// www.healthyplace.com/addictions/ addictions-information/ types-of-addiction-list-of-addictions/.

The Diagnostic and Statistical Manual of Mental Disorders (DSM) IV–TR provides a list of addictions relating to the following substances:

- alcohol
- tobacco
- opioids (like heroin)
- prescription drugs (sedatives, hypnotics, or anxiolytics like sleeping pills and tranquilizers)
- cocaine

- cannabis (marijuana)
- amphetamines (like methamphetamine, known as meth)
- hallucinogens
- inhalants
- phencyclidine (known as PCP or angel dust)
- other unspecified substances

A list of impulse control disorders is presented below (http://www. healthyplace.com/ addictions/addictions-information/types-of-addiction-list-of-addictions/). We must first understand the DSM IV–TR lists disorders where impulses cannot be resisted, which could be considered a type of addiction. The following is a list of the recognized impulse control disorders:

- intermittent explosive disorder (compulsive aggressive and assaultive acts)
- kleptomania (compulsive stealing)
- pyromania (compulsive setting of fires)
- gambling

A list of addictions is also listed at (http://www. healthyplace. com/addictions/addictions-information/types-of-addiction-list-of-addictions/); some of these are listed below. First, it has been suggested one of the types of addiction is known as behavioural addiction. The following is a list of these behaviors that have been noted to be addictive:

- food (eating)
- sex
- pornography (attaining, viewing)
- using computers and the internet
- playing video games
- working
- exercising
- spiritual obsession (as opposed to religious devotion)
- pain (seeking)

- cutting
- shopping

How many people are dealing with addictions?

One in ten US adults was at one time in recovery from drug or alcohol, according to a new survey (http://www.huffingtonpost. com/ 2012/03/07/addiction-recovery-america-drugs-alcohol_n_ 1327344. html). The new report, by the Partnership at Drugfree.org and the New York State Office of Alcoholism and Substance Abuse Services, shows that there are as many as 23.5 million adults in the US who have at one time had issues with their alcohol consumption or drug use.

Getting Help for an Addiction

There are many organizations that provide help in treating addictions. Your primary care provider is a good point of contact. He or she will be able to provide you with help and advice and can recommend specialists and addiction services, both nationally and locally (http://www. wisegeek.org/what-is-the-golden-rule. htm#did youknowoutist).

Treatment for addiction focuses on the individual and his or her needs. Various forms of therapy and medication are recommended treatments. The most effective forms of therapy for treating addiction include the following:

- individual counseling
- group counseling
- twelve-step programs
- family therapy
- Christian counseling
- medications

Here are recommended resources for getting help with addictions:

Sources of Recovery Information

- Addiction Recovery Guide: http:// www.addictionrecovery guide.org/
- Addictions and Recovery: http://addictionsandrecovery.org
- The Association of Lesbian, Gay, Bisexual, Transgender Addiction Professionals and Their Allies (NALGAP): http://www.nalgap.org
- Faces and Voices of Recovery:
  - o http://www.facesandvoicesofrecovery.org/
and
  - o http://www.facesandvoicesofrecovery.org/resources/international/International.php
- Helping Others Live Sober: http:// www.helpingotherslive sober.org/
- National Alliance for Medication Assisted Recovery: http:// methadone. org
- National Association of Recovery Residences (NARR): http:// narronline.com

Resources for Addiction Recovery Support

- National Council on Alcoholism and Drug Dependence, Inc. (NCADD) Recovery Support: http://ncadd.org/index.php/recovery-support/overview
- Substance Abuse and Mental Health Services Administration (SAMHSA) Recovery Support: http://www.samhsa.gov/recovery/
- Partners for Recovery: http://partnersforrecovery.samhsa.gov/
- National Recovery Month: http://www.recoverymonth.gov/
- Women for Sobriety: http://womenforsobriety.org
- Faces and Voices of Recovery: http://www.facesandvoicesof recovery.org/

- Helping Others Live Sober: http://www.helpingotherslive sober.org/
- National Alliance for Medication Assisted Recovery: http://methadone.org
- National Association of Recovery Residences (NARR): http://narronline.com

Resources for Addiction Recovery Support

- National Council on Alcoholism and Drug Dependence, Inc. (NCADD) Recovery Support: http://ncadd.org/index.php/recovery-support/overview
- Substance Abuse and Mental Health Services Administration (SAMHSA) Recovery Support: http://www.samhsa. gov/recovery/

Recommended Resources

The following additional resources will help you get a good start on getting healthy and fit.

The Internet

- American Heart Association n.d.). Getting healthy. Retrieved from http://www. heart.org/HEARTORG/GettingHealthy/GettingHealthy_UCM_001078_SubHomePage.jsp
- Gold, S. S. (2015). *Twenty quick and easy ways to get healthier fast.* Retrieved from http://www.health.com/health/gallery/0,20668027,00.html
- Hatti, M. (2015). Healthy living: Eight steps to take today. Retrieved from http://www. webmd.com/balance/features/healthy-living-8-steps-to-take-today
- March of Dimes Foundation. (2015). Getting healthy before pregnancy test. Retrieved from http://www.marchofdimes. org/ pregnancy/getting-healthy-before-pregnancy.aspx

Books

- Clemens, M. (2010). *Think and grow fit: A rational person's guide to getting fit and staying that way forever.* Publisher: Universe.
- Crowley, C., & Lodge, H. S. (2007). *Younger next year for women: Live strong, fit, and sexy—Until you're eighty and beyond.* Publisher: Workman.
- Hahn, F. (2008). *Strong kids, healthy kids: The revolutionary program for increasing your child's fitness in thirty minutes a week.* Publisher: AMACOM.
- Matthews, M. (2015). *Thinner leaner strong: The simple science of building the ultimate body.* Publisher: Oculus.
- Scholar, G. (2010). *Fit nurse: Your total plan for getting fit and living well.* Publisher: Sigma Theta Tau.

Personal Notes from the Author

"If I could Turn Back the Hands of Time" comes to my mind when I think about addictions. I would have lived my life in a healthier way. I have had a lifetime battle with my weight. I have had the problem over too many decades. I should have invested in psychiatric treatments to get to the root of my problem. One thing for sure is that I was not taught good diet and exercise habits at a young age.

Children should be taught good diet and exercise habits at a very young age. It is hard to change diet and exercise habits when you get older. It gets worse. I failed at teaching and demonstrating good, healthy habits before my children. You have to teach and demonstrate healthy habits. Not only do children listen to what you say, but they also watch what you do. Now my daughters are dealing with weight issues. Hopefully, my grandchildren and future descendants will have a better start. It is never too late to end a family curse.

CHAPTER 7

Getting Smart about Your Faith

To one who has faith, no explanation is necessary.
To one without faith, no explanation is possible.

—Thomas Aquinas

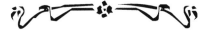

We live in a country where we have the freedom to worship as we choose. We can choose or refrain from religion. I have found that people who do not have faith make bad choices, give up easily, have limited abilities to fight challenges, and are unhappy. We have to believe that there is a power greater than ourselves. It is really foolish to look at creation and not believe or recognize that there is a power or something greater than all of us.

Why Do We Need Faith?

According to M. Farouk Radwan (2015), there are three reasons we need faith:

- "To be able to think positively" (http://www.2knowmyself. com/why_do_we_need_faith). If you expect good things to happen, they will. This is one of the keys to success. At the same time, you will need a realistic plan and proven data to show that it works. It is safe to have a plan A and plan B. It is positive to keep trying even if you have to change paths.

You have the confirmation from your higher power that you are somebody and have the right to be happy, successful, and prosperous.

- "To be sure that you are going to win." As stated earlier, it is all about your belief systems. Do you believe in a higher power who has given you a stamp of approval to win over life issues? Do you believe that you are worthy of winning? Putting these together will get you to the winning path.

- "To feel good during down times." Everybody has good days and bad days. We have successes and failures. It is what life is all about. How you deal with these challenges sets the stage for your happiness or unhappiness. A faith in a higher power gives you the support needed to get through the low times of life.

Dealing with Stress

According to the Faith and Health Connection (2015), many people use food as a way to cope with stress (http://www.faithandhealth connection.org/). Yet, others use drugs, turn to alcohol, or light up a cigarette. Some burn the midnight oil surfing the Internet and pay for it the next day because they have had inadequate sleep.

Faith and Health Connection also informs us that faith can be the anchor that keeps a person steady in times of stress. If followed, biblical principles can be the cornerstone of a person's life and enable him or her to live a life less impacted by what otherwise would be stressful circumstances.

Taking the Focus off You

Sometimes, we get caught up in ourselves. Too much focus on ourselves can lead to harsh self- evaluation, unforgiveness of ourselves and others, and decreased love for ourselves. It is easy to become depressed when you are focusing on your failures and negative traits. We should never evaluate ourselves based on other people's attributes. This can lead to further depression. It can also lead to decreased self-love.

I worked many years as a mental health counselor. I have emphasized to clients that they should find another focus. When you sit around all day thinking about your "haves and have nots," you can get really down. When you get involved in a local church, helping others, and spending quality time with family and friends, you can become a different person.

We all make errors of some kind. We learn from these and should move on. This begins with forgiving ourselves. At the same time, we should forgive others for their errors toward us. Unforgiveness blocks you from moving forward. You can get stuck. In fact, the person that you cannot forgive is moving on with his or her life. You are the only one stuck. You cannot spend your time and energy focusing on these negative activities. You will fall behind in your psychological and spiritual growth and development.

Your faith is your key to success. It gives you a reason to get up every morning or day. It also gives you a positive attitude and the assurance that you will be successful, safe, healthy, and wealthy. It further gives you a positive feeling about interacting with people. You will not feel that everybody is evil and wanting to hurt and insult you. However, you must use wisdom as you interact with people. There are some people you must avoid.

Faith helps you to set your priorities in order. Religion is one vehicle for developing faith. Most religions teach us about moral and ethical behavior. I love the "Golden Rule" principle. It commands us to treat others as we wish to be treated. In the Christian faith, the rule was developed from this Bible verse: "So whatever you wish that others would do to you, do also to them, for this is the Law and the Prophets" (Matthew 7:12, English Standard Version). There are many other verses that teach us proper conduct.

Religion versus Spirituality

There are several articles that attempt to help us to understand the difference between religion and spirituality. The first article was written by the Compelling Truth (2016) (http://www.compellingtruth.org/difference-religion-spirituality.html). The difference was described in this way:

> Religion and spirituality are two related yet distinct terms associated with faith. *Religion* denotes "a set of beliefs concerning the cause, nature, and purpose of the universe, usually involving devotional and ritual observances and a moral code." In contrast, *spirituality* can be defined as "the quality of being spiritual" (both definitions adapted from www.dictionary.com).
>
> Based on these definitions, the major difference between religion and spirituality is one of *believing* versus *being*. Religion's focus is the content of one's belief and the outworking of that belief; spirituality's focus is the process of becoming more attuned to unworldly affairs.

It is easy to see that it is possible to be religious without being spiritual and spiritual without being religious.

A religious person accepts a certain set of beliefs as true and observes a certain set of rituals. A person of the Christian religion believes Jesus is God's Son and observes baptism and Communion. A person of the Muslim religion believes Allah is God and observes Ramadan and *salat*.

In a different perspective, spirituality is the fact of being spiritual and is usually evidenced by the act of doing spiritual things. Praying, meditating, reading Scripture, and giving to a charity are all things that a "spiritual" person might do.

In another article by Shapiro (2012), the difference between religion and spirituality is described. According to this article,

> Religion is often about who's in and who's out, creating a worldview steeped in "us against them." Spirituality rejects this dualism and speaks of us and

them. Religion is often about loyalty to institutions, clergy, and rules. Spirituality is about loyalty to justice and compassion. Religion talks about God. Spirituality helps to make us godly. The two need not be at odds. Religion at its best is spirituality in community (https:// spiritualityhealth.com/articles/ what-difference-between-religion-and-spirituality).

Additionally, in another article by the World Blessings (2015), the difference between religion and spirituality was also discussed (http://www. worldblessings.com/). This includes these definitions:

Religion can be seen as a pathway that leads to God. The pathway is not God, but in the best and highest intentions it would lead people closer to God. All true religious paths and teachings came into existence through divine inspiration and revelation, the spark of God's love and light that opens a pathway for God's presence to be seen and felt more directly.

Spirituality is a more general term that includes religion but that also encompasses the general human impulse to reach out towards the greater whole of which we all are a part. The difference between religion and spirituality is simply that most religions offer a specific set of beliefs and structures to help people to attune to their innate spirituality (http:// www.worldblessings.com/ difference-between-religion-and-spirituality. html#ixzz3nQGiN3J3).

We can basically conclude that one can be both religious and spiritual at the same time. You can be spiritual without being religious. The focus is on what you perceive as your source of spirituality.

According to the Regents of California's article entitled "Spiritual Wellness" (http://wellness. ucr.edu/spiritual_wellness.html),

The path to spiritual wellness may involve meditation, prayer, affirmations, or specific spiritual practices that support your connection to a higher power or belief system.

Compassion, the capacity for love and forgiveness, altruism, joy, and fulfillment help you enjoy your spiritual health. Your religious faith, values, beliefs, principles, and morals define your spirituality.

If you are a person engaged in the process of spiritual wellness, you are willing and able to transcend yourself in order to question the meaning and purpose in your life and the lives of others. In addition, you seek to find harmony between that which lies within and the social and physical forces that come from outside.

According to the University of New Hampshire Health Services, signs of spiritual wellness include the following (http:// www. unh.edu/health-services/ohep/spiritual-wellness):

- development of a purpose in life,
- ability to spend reflective time alone,
- taking time to reflect on the meaning of events in life,
- having a clear sense of right and wrong, and acting accordingly,
- having the ability to explain why you believe what you believe,
- caring and acting for the welfare of others and the environment,
- being able to practice forgiveness and compassion in life.

To help you with your spiritual journey, the following resources are recommended:

The Internet

- Wellness: Spiritual Wellness. (2014). Retrieved from http:// wellness.ucr.edu/ spiritual_wellness.html

- Perkins, C. (2015). Spiritual Health. Retrieved from http://www. holistichelp.net/spiritual-health.html
- Kurus, M. (2015). Physical, Emotional, Mental, and Spiritual Health. Retrieved from http://www.mkprojects. com/fa_PEMHealth.htm
- Stalnacke, M-A. (2011). Top Ten Ways to Boost Spiritual Health. Retrieved from http://www.christianpost.com/ news/top-10-ways-to-boost-spiritual-health-51322/
- The Nemours Foundations. (2015). How Can Spirituality Affect Your Family's Health? Retrieved from http:// kidshealth. org/parent/emotions/feelings/spirituality.html

Books

- The Holy Bible
- Boatmon, L. M. (2009). *Workout and worship: Eight steps to physical and spiritual health.* Publisher: iUniverse.
- Luo, V. P., & Hill, D. (2010). *Spiritual and healing: The art of living.* Publisher: Trafford.
- Meyer, J. (2014). *Good health, good life: Twelve keys to enjoying physical and spiritual wellness.* Publisher: FaithWork.
- Paprock, J. (2012). *Seven keys to spiritual wellness: Enriching your faith by strengthening the health of your soul.* Publisher: Loyola.
- Price, C. S. (2010). *Spiritual and physical Health.* Publisher: Kessinger.

Personal Notes from the Author

In my case, I believe in God and try to live by religious principles taught in the Bible. I do spiritual activities, such as praying, mediating, fasting, Bible study, and being fair and caring toward others. I have learned over the years that we must work hard to maintain our spiritual health.

As I get older, I get better at taking care of my spiritual health. As a result, I have become calmer about my life. I am not always in a hurry. There is less chaos. I am more forgiving and tolerant of others. All of these give me great pleasure and peace about my life. Most importantly, I have learned to forgive myself.

CHAPTER 8

Getting Smart about Your Education

If you always put limits on what you can do, physical or anything else, it'll spread over into the rest of your life. It'll spread into your work, into your morality, into your entire being. There are no limits. There are plateaus, but you must not stay there, you must go beyond them. If it kills you, it kills you. A man must constantly exceed his level.

—Bruce Lee, *The Art of Expressing the Human Body*

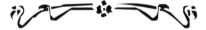

E ducation is the key to success in many aspects of your life. Education will help you to gain employment and a good income. The quality and type of education can change your station in life, especially when you come from poverty. Education can help you to have more compassion for humankind, change your worldview, and help you to communicate through multimedia.

What Does It Mean to Be Educated?

Denning (2011) suggests that the characteristics of being educated include a demonstrated ability to listen carefully, to think critically, to evaluate facts rigorously, to reason analytically, to imagine creatively, to articulate interesting questions, to explore alternative viewpoints, to maintain intellectual curiosity, and to speak and write persuasively. If we add to that a reasonable familiarity with the treasures of history, literature, theater, music, dance, and art that previous civilizations have delivered, we are getting to close to the meaning of educated (http://www. forbes.com/ sites/stevedenning/ 2011/07/31/what-does-it-mean-to-be-educated/).

Why Should You Get Educated?

According to Lucier (2015), there are several reasons why we should get a college degree. (http://collegelife.about.com/od/ academiclife/a/ 10ReasonstoGetADegree.htm). She divides these reasons into two categories: tangible reasons and intangible reasons.

Tangible Reasons to Get a College Degree

1. You will make more money.
2. You will have a lifetime of increased opportunities.
3. You will be more empowered as an agent in your own life.
4. You will be better able to weather adversity.
5. You will always be marketable.

Intangible Reasons to Get a College Degree

1. You will lead a more examined life.
2. You can be an agent of change for others.
3. You will have more access to resources.
4. You will have future opportunities in ways you may not be considering now.
5. You will have a strong sense of pride and self.

It cannot be overemphasized that an education is the best way out of poverty. People who have famous and rich parents have other options. They get a head start in their parents' businesses or industries. If a highly-specialized skill is required, it will be necessary for them to go college. For example, a law or medical degree may be required to work as a professional in the parents' offices. Otherwise, these parents can hire them in other capacities. It is really hard for poor people to work their way out of their circumstances. Education is essential for this change in this circumstance.

You would agree that the best time to get an education is when you are young. Life happens and it is never too late. It does not matter what your circumstances are. You must make up your mind to get your education. Nothing can stop you. It is all about what you want. There are people who will be able to help you with your educational plan. It is recommended that you seek these resources. These resources can be former teachers and principals, your pastors, community leaders, and people that you admire. Most people are willing to help. It is up to you to take this first step.

You must decide on what career you want. You will begin by examining your personality type. Do you like working with people? Do you work best alone? Do you like helping people, and in what capacity? How important is service type work to you? Is money more important? These are some of the questions that you must address.

Next, it is suggested that you search the career market. Look in the newspaper under the employment section. Look online at Monster, Indeed, Simplyhired, and others. This research gives you a hint on what jobs are needed.

Finally, find the college that offers the programs for your career interest. Start with the local community colleges. "Community colleges, sometimes called junior colleges, technical colleges, two-year colleges, or city colleges, are primarily two-year public institutions providing higher education and lower-level tertiary education, granting certificates, diplomas, and associate's degrees. Many also offer continuing and adult education. After graduating from a community college, some students transfer to a four-year liberal arts college or university for two to three years to complete a bachelor's degree" (https://en. wikipedia.org/wiki/ Community_college).

Depending on your career goals, a bachelor's degree may be

required. It is then necessary to check out the local colleges and universities that offer your future major. You can go online to check out your school of choice. Some libraries have hard copies of college catalogs on hand. Things have become very high-tech, so you may expect to see limited to no hard copies available. All colleges have catalogs online at their websites.

Finally, you must visit the colleges that you are interested in attending. All of them are willing to help you. Call and make an appointment. They will help with your admission application, financial process, and housing.

Here is list of recommendations to help your journey in returning to school.

The Internet

- Six financial benefits of a college degree. (2015). Retrieved from http://collegelife. about.com/od/academiclife/a/6Fin ancialBenefitsOfACollegeDegree.htm
- How to choose your college major. (2015). Retrieved from http://collegelife.about. com/od/academiclife/a/ pickingamajor.htm
- Caldwell, M. (2015). Should I go back to get an undergraduate degree? Retrieved from http://moneyfor20s.about.com/od/ studentloans/f/Should_I_go_back_to_school.htm
- How to pass a college class. (2015). Retrieved from http:// collegelife.about.com/ od/academiclife/fl/How-to-Pass-a-College-Class.htm
- Ten things to know about your college classes. (2015). Retrieved from http://collegelife.about.com/od/academiclife/ fl/10-Things-to-Know-About-Your-College-Classes.htm
- How to pick your college classes. (2015). Retrieved from http://collegelife.about.com/ od/academiclife/a/picking courses.htm

Books

- Babb, D. (2013). *The adult student: An insider's guide to going back to school.* Publisher: Mandeville.
- Gibson, S. U., & Gibson, J. R. (2007). *Making As in college: What smart students know: The study—professor's guide, kindle.* Publisher: Workbooks.
- Siebert, A., & Karrm, N. (2008). *The adult student's guide to survival and success.* Publisher: Practical Psychology Press.
- Snyder, A. (2013). *Going back to college—continuing education as an adult.* Publisher: Snyder.
- Tanabe, G., & Tanabe, K. (2007). *Adult students: A painless guide to going back to college.* Publisher: Supercollege, LLC.

Personal Notes from the Author

I was taught at an early age to seek an education. It was important to my parents that we get a good education. They wanted their two daughters to have a decent education and a decent and respectable job. They did not want us to do manual labor or housekeeping work. They often said that manual labor and housekeeping should be done at our own homes.

I am glad that I listened. As I told you earlier, I am a single parent and grandparent. As a result, I had to care for my children all by myself. I did not get any help from their father. Because of my level of education, I was able to establish a successful career and earn a good salary. I was able to help my younger daughter to get her bachelor's and master's degrees in mechanical engineering. My older is a registered nurse at the associate degree level. She recently earned her bachelor's degree in nursing and has plans for master's degree in a family nurse practitioner program. They are also single parents. I pray that they will be able to care for their children alone should it become necessary.

CHAPTER 9

Getting Smart about Your Career

Accept responsibility for your life.
Know that it is you who will get you
where you want to go, no one else.

—Les Brown, *Live Your Dreams*

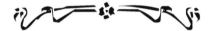

The role of women has significantly changed over the years. Most women have to work outside the home. According to Lodge (2014) in *Fortune,* "Breadwinner moms in the United States make up nearly half of households' major earners or are on par income-wise with their significant others, according to a new study." She further stated that this represents about a 10 percent jump from a year ago, when Pew Research released a report that four in ten or 40 percent, of US working moms were reported to be their families' primary providers (http://fortune.com/ 2014/11/03/ female-breadwinners/).

Women have a choice to work outside of the home. It is simply a beautiful thing that women have this choice. Some women have to work outside the home in order to survive. Hitti (2007) took a look at the findings of a poll which was designed to determine whether women would prefer to work outside the home. According to Hitti's analysis of the poll, "Among women, 58 percent said they would prefer to work outside the home, 37 percent indicated that they would rather stay at home, three percent (3%) said they wanted to do both, and two percent (two%) expressed no opinion" (http://www.webmd.com/women/ news/20070906/women-prefer-working-outside-the-home). Additionally, she reported that "the percentage of women who would prefer working outside the home is slightly higher than the 54 percent who voiced that preference two years ago."

The purpose of this chapter is not to argue whether these women are correct or not. The purpose of this chapter is to help women who are interested in seeking a career to take full advantages of the opportunities available to them in the workforce. The first point is that women should know the difference between having a job and having a career.

Basically, a career is the pursuit of a lifelong ambition or the general course of progression toward lifelong goals, whereas a job is an activity through which an individual can earn money. It is a regular activity in exchange for payment (http:// www.diffen.com/difference/Career_vs_Job).

According to an article published at http://www.difference between.net/business/difference-between-job-and-career/, there is another difference between having a job and having a career. The article stated that a person with a job "is concerned about getting a steady paycheck." This person "will do those things required to keep receiving that paycheck: show up on time, complete all his tasks satisfactorily, and get along with his coworkers and boss." A person with a career is one who "wants to learn more about his career and network with his colleagues to create further opportunities." A career-oriented person "is willing to take risks to further himself. He is more concerned with job satisfaction and pay is secondary."

Most women who have to work or prefer to work will find a career more satisfying that a job. At the same time, people view their careers as life-long endeavors. While they might not plan to be at the same company, they hope to do the same type of work until they retire. Many career-minded people continue with their careers as consultants or advisors after they officially retire.

Roth (2008) does a great job in helping us to understand the difference between a job and career. He listed the following differences (http://www. getrichslowly.org/blog/2008/07/10/the-difference-between-a-career-and-a-job/):

- "A job is something you do simply to earn money; a career is a series of connected employment opportunities."
- "A job has minimal impact on your future work life, while a career provides experience and learning to fuel your future."
- "A job offers few networking opportunities, but a career is loaded with them."
- "When you work at a job, you should do the minimum without annoying the boss. When you're in a career, you should go the extra mile, doing tasks beyond your minimum job description."

Now you must decide whether you want to have a job or a career. It is somewhat easier to find a job. You ask family and friends, attend job fairs, register with the employment services in your hometown, and do a search in the newspaper or on the Internet. A career is different. According to McKay (2015), there are hundreds of career options out there (http://careerplanning.about.com). She offered several important steps:

- "Assess yourself." Your values, interests, and skills, in combination with certain personality, will make some careers especially suitable for you and others particularly inappropriate. There are a number of assessment tools out there. Career counselors, school counselors, employment agencies, and other related professionals can offer good advice. Also, there are a number of books and articles in magazines and on the internet that can help with making this decision.
- "Make a list of occupations to explore." List the types of jobs you would like to have. Can these jobs be grouped together as a career? For example, if you like taking care of sick people, what kinds of jobs would you like to do to help sick people? What careers would enable you to take

care of sick people? Would you like to be a nurse, physician, physical therapist, or another type of therapist? As you narrow your options, evaluate yourself in relation to the career options. For example, would you rather work at the bedside or in a clinic?

- "Explore the occupations on your list." You need to learn a lot about these options that you have chosen. You will need to know the job description, educational requirements, other requirements, job outlook, advancement opportunities, and salaries.
- "Continue narrowing down your list." Based on your findings from the above research, you should have an idea of what you would rather do. Mark off those items that fit you.
- "Conduct informational interviews." Find people who do this work. Ask them about their work, about how they got started, about their job satisfactions, and job dissatisfactions.
- "Set your goals," Now that you have selected a career, it is time to set your goal(s). What do you hope to achieve and when?
- "Write a career action plan." What are the steps involved in becoming a successful person in your chosen career? "A career action plan will help guide you as you pursue your long- and short-term goals."
- "Train for your new career." Depending on your career choice, you may have to attend college, a vocational school, graduate school or a professional school. You may have to do an internship or gain specific work experience.

Recommended Resources

Internet Searches

- http://www.careerbuilder.com/jobs/keyword/magazine/
- http://www.magazine.org/magazine-careers
- http://www.jobsandcareersmag.com
- http://www.bls.gov/ooh/
- http://careeroutlook.us/

- http://www.careerplanner.com/Job-Outlook-Index.cfm
- http://joboutlook.gov.au/

Books

- Crompton, D. (2010). *Find a job through social networking.* JIST Publishing.
- Hewlett, S.A. (2013). *Forget a mentor, find a sponsor: The new way to fast-track your career.* Harvard Business Review Press.
- Lore, N. (2012). *The pathfinder: How to choose or change your career for a lifetime of satisfaction and success.* Touchstone Publisher.
- Umber, J. (2015). *Find your passion: Five questions to ask yourself that will help you find your purpose in as little as one hour.* SouthShore Publications.
- Wagele, E., & Stabb, I. (2009). *The career within you: How to find the perfect job for your personality.* Harper One Publisher.
- Zichy, S., & Bidou, A. (2007). *Career match: Connecting who you are with what you'll love to do.* AMACOM Publishers.

Personal Notes from the Author

I have found it to be very rewarding to have a career. I am one of those women who had to work. Working a bunch of unrelated jobs was not appealing to me. From a very young age, I wanted to be a teacher. I have changed my disciplines of interest several times while in school. After becoming a teacher, I have entirely changed disciplines. Therefore, my teaching career has been in two disciplines, education and nursing.

My nursing started as a desire for a part-time job to supplement my teaching income. As a single parent, I need extra income to increase my abilities to offer my daughters just something extra, such as dance lessons, piano and one other instrument lessons, travel, and other things to enhance their backgrounds.

After making a decision to learn new skills to meet my goal, I was working at a university, where I taught education, psychology, and reading courses. I studied the university catalog, looked at job and occupation outlook information, and interviewed people. I came to the conclusion that nursing was my best choice. Consequently, I earned another bachelor's degree. My career expansion was nursing. Later, I decided nursing was a great fit for me. I earned a master's degree in nursing. At that point, I changed my career to teaching and practicing nursing. Now, I am currently pursuing a doctorate of nursing degree. It was a great combination for me and my family.

You can have a career, too. It requires an informed decision. You will begin with a study of your chosen career options. Next, make a decision. Then you determine your goal(s) and make a plan. Finally, you implement your plan and enjoy your career. You can do this. Have faith and ask for the guidance from your higher power.

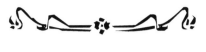

CHAPTER 10

Getting Smart about Child-Rearing

The attitude you have as a parent is what your
kids will learn from more than what you tell
them. They don't remember what you try to
teach them. They remember what you are.

—Jim Henson

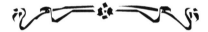

O ne of the most important jobs given to a human being is
caring for children. Humans differ from other animals. It
takes longer to care for an offspring until full adulthood.
In addition to your children's survival skills, you must teach your
children good decision-making skills, problem-solving skills, and
critical thinking skills. Humans have a unique gift to think through
problems as compared to animals, whose behavior is the result of
instinct. Instinct does not work well with people. People must
behave logically. It takes a while to get children to this level.

In order for children to develop properly, they must be
loved unconditionally, receive positive regard from parents and
significant others, and live in a positive environment. There is no
perfect setting; however, there must be significant efforts toward
setting a good stage for positive growth. This would include having
supportive parents, helping the children to have a high sense of self-
worthiness, giving them unconditional acceptance, and providing
an environment free of abuse and violence.

Parents must value education and teach their children to value education. They must positively reinforce the child's efforts to succeed in learning. Parents demonstrate the proper behaviors for the child to learn. For example, children must see their parents reading and advancing their education.

Parents have the awesome task of teaching religious and spiritual concepts. The children learn this best by modeling and imitation. These lessons are no longer expected in public schools. In fact, it is against the law to engage in these activities. Parents and churches have the full responsibility for teaching religious principles. Schools can teach spiritual principles that do not have a religious undertone. These would include having compassion for others, having the ability to love and forgive, altruism, joy, and fulfillment.

Respect for self and others is first learned from parents. Parents who do not respect authority and other valuable institutions will have children who disrespect authority and other institutions, themselves, and others. Disrespectful children will have a poor outlook for success in school and higher education, on a job, and in their chosen careers.

Children learn about love, relationships, family dynamics, marriage, courting, and other social skills from their parents. This author has worked many years in mental health. During these times, she has seen over and over that people who have problems in these areas have parents who have problems in the same areas. This does not mean that every disturbed child has a disturbed parent or family, but more often than not, it is true.

Children learn how to communicate from parents and family. If children are encouraged to communicate their thoughts and feelings, they learn to express themselves and tolerate other people's thoughts and feelings. Family secrets can lead to all levels of dysfunction. First, we must realize that every family has its secrets; however, it is the content of the secret that makes the problem. For example, sexual abuse, domestic violence, and other forms of abuse are kept secret in families. Handler (2013) identified "Five Reasons Why Keeping Family Secrets Could Be Harmful" (http:// psychcentral.com/blog/archives/

2013/08/22/5-reasons-why-keeping-family-secrets-could-be-harmful/). These include:

- "Keeping secrets can destroy relationships." Communication becomes limited because feelings cannot be discussed. This negatively impacts family relationships.
- "Keeping secrets can affect children's lives." Children will learn that the secret activities are normal and do not realize that they have negative outcomes due to the abuse. They will later learn that their family was different in a negative way.
- "Keeping secrets can create a false sense of reality. Children judge the real world by what they are taught at home. The shock comes when they realize that what they had learned is not true or is not normal."
- "Keeping secrets can cause illness." According to Handle, "keeping traumatic secrets can result in excessive stress and guilt for the person carrying the burden of knowledge, even when that silence is thought to be the best possible option for all concerned. Physical symptoms such as anxiety, headaches, backaches, and digestive problems often can occur when disturbing secrets are internalized, rather than shared, especially over a long period of time."

Personal Notes from the Author

One of the hardest challenges that I have ever encountered was rearing my children as a single parent. I do not recommend single parenthood. Sometimes, things happen, and we must roll with the flow. I never wanted a divorce. I grew up in a two-parent home and wanted that for my children. There comes a time to decide what is best for yourself and your children.

Verbal and physical abuse should not be tolerated in any home. Children who live with and see violence grow up to violence. You can be in a situation where there are attempts to injure self-esteem and self-worth. This also becomes a time to seek counseling and other remedies. Divorce is unfortunate. But it happens.

Caring for children requires a lot of sacrifice and selfless work. When the children are grown, you will have great pride. By the way, God recognizes rearing children as a blessing and ministry. This is illustrated in these verses from the Bible:

- Psalm 127:3–5 (ESV): "Behold, children are a heritage from the Lord, the fruit of the womb a reward. Like arrows in the hand of a warrior are the children of one's youth. Blessed is the man who fills his quiver with them! He shall not be put to shame when he speaks with his enemies in the gate."

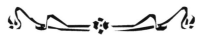

CHAPTER 11

Now It Is Up to You

If you try anything, if you try to lose weight, or
to improve yourself, or to love, or to make the
world a better place, you have already achieved
something wonderful, before you even begin.
Forget failure. If things don't work out the
way you want, hold your head up high and be
proud. And try again. And again. And again!

—Sarah Dessen, *Keeping the Moon*

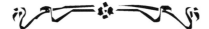

God has given all of us the freedom of choice. He has given
us the responsibility to make good decisions, and we must
accept the consequences of our decisions. It is so very
important to make informed decisions. It is dangerous to make
decisions too fast without the appropriate facts.

You can never have all of the information that you need to make
a sound decision. At the same time, you may find it necessary to
delay making a decision while trying to gather information. This is
the time we must prayerfully seek guidance from a higher power.
This quote says it better and straight to the point:

On an important decision one rarely has 100 percent
of the information needed for a good decision no
matter how much one spends or how long one waits.

And, if one waits too long, he has a different problem and has to start all over. This is the terrible dilemma of the hesitant decision maker.

—Robert K. Greenleaf, *Servant As Leader*

We are expected to exercise wisdom in our decision-making. In order to do this, we must observe our environments, study various resources, pray, mediate, and talk with people who have achieved similar goals.

Change is hard for many people. We must see change as a positive event. We can get past our pain associated with change. It is essential for achieving success.

> *Getting over a painful experience is much*
> *like crossing monkey bars. You have to let go*
> *at some point in order to move forward.*
>
> —C.S. Lewis

People claim to not have enough time to do what they need to do. This is simply an excuse. I cannot say this better than the quote below.

> *Don't say you don't have enough time. You*
> *have exactly the same number of hours per*
> *day that were given to Helen Keller, Pasteur,*
> *Michelangelo, Mother Teresea, Leonardo da*
> *Vinci, Thomas Jefferson, and Albert Einstein.*
>
> —*Life's Little Instruction Book*

You cannot let the past pains in your life control the rest of your life. Everybody living has gone through something. It is all about your attitude, faith, and willingness to move forward.

> *Someone was hurt before you, wronged before*
> *you, hungry before you, frightened before you,*

> *beaten before you, humiliated before you,*
> *raped before you ... yet, someone survived ...*
> *You can do anything you choose to do.*

—Maya Angelou

Remember to be honest in all of your dealings with others. When you give your word, you must stand by it. Most importantly, do not cheat others. According to Paige (2015), "honest business practices inspire staff and customers with respect for your mission. Honest business practices build foundations of trust with colleagues, competitors, staff, customers, and every other individual and entity. When employers deal honestly with their staff, employees are motivated to drive the business forward. Creditors and investors express confidence by funding company development and consumer confidence is positive" (http://smallbusiness.chron. com/honesty-important-business-22624.html). As you can easily see, there are advantages to being honest in your future endeavors.

Being honest with people is the application of the Golden Rule. "Treating employees, partners, investors, and customers in the ways the business owner would want them to treat him creates an environment of trust and support. An owner can resist the short-term gratification at the expense of long-term commitment to the web of relationships in which his business is involved. He can avoid the blinding trap that crops up when dishonesty clouds perception. The Golden Rule helps to diminish greed, envy, and the actions that accompany those less than virtuous qualities" (Paige, 2015, http:// smallbusiness. chron.com/honesty-important-business-2624.html).

Respect for others is another key to success. Shalman (2007) describes the behaviors that demonstrate respect. Showing respect, according to Shalman, includes the following (http://www. alexshalman. com/ 2007/09/18/10-ways-to-show-respect/):

1. Listen harder.
2. Be considerate.
3. Keep your promise.
4. Be on time.

5. Have manners.
6. Encourage.
7. Be fair.
8. Go out of your way.
9. Preserve dignity.
10. Do not assume. Do not assume anything about a person based on the person's race, income level, or gender. Start off each interaction by thinking of the other person as your equal.

You have been provided with the basic information to build additional positive outcomes for your life and for your children. It is up to you to step out on faith.

> *You may not be able to see the sun in your life right now, but that doesn't mean it's not up there. The clouds will not last forever. The sun will shine in your life once again. Just stay in faith and believe in God. He'll meet all your needs, he'll fulfill all your dreams, and he'll answer all your prayers. Don't give up. Just be with hope that God will change your life someday.*

—Unknown Author

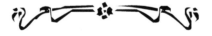

Printed in the United States
By Bookmasters